HOW TO READ
FICTION

By

GORDON HALL GEROULD

NEW YORK / RUSSELL & RUSSELL

PREFACE

Although a great deal has been written about fiction, too little attention has been paid to the reader's connection with it. Yet everyone agrees, I suppose, that no transaction in the arts is complete until at least one other person receives what the creator has imagined and tried to communicate. The play implies an audience, and so does every tale. In the following chapters I have attempted, therefore, to look at the art of story-telling from the point of view of the reader. I have drawn relatively few of my illustrations from recent books, not because I lack interest in them, but because I did not wish to appear to be undertaking the enormously difficult task of writing a guide to contemporary fiction. I have tried to keep my attention on fundamental things, and on what any intelligent person should look for in stories whether old or new. In a word, what follows is not literary history or a statement of literary judgments, but merely a little treatise on the art of reading fiction.

CONTENTS

(1)

The Variety of Prose Fiction

MOST readers of fiction—and nearly everyone who reads at all does read fiction—ask
only two questions about a book. They inquire: Is
it interesting? Is it real? and are satisfied, if bewildered, by the conflicting answers they receive.
One group of friends and most reviewers assure
them that the story is enthralling and amazingly
true to life; another set of friends and a sprinkling
of reviewers find it rather dull and strained. Unless
too much discouraged, the undiscriminating
reader gets the book, gulps it down, and joins
heartily in the chorus of condemnation or praise,
though he knows no better than before why it
interests him or how to estimate the truth that is
in it.

The questions that he asks, and often cannot
answer, are perfectly legitimate ones; but adequate

replies need thought. Yes or no will not do. The story may be interesting in many quite different ways, which must be stated; or it may be tedious for many different reasons. Perhaps the interest may lie in an ingenious plot, or it may come from the skill with which a group of people is pictured, or it may rest on the subtlety with which the minds of two or three individuals are probed, or it may make a forthright assault on our emotions. Seldom will it be interesting in all these ways at once. Similarly a story may deserve to be called real in almost as many ways as there are individual writers with the power to observe life with true insight and fresh imagination; and it may be false in even more ways, since most authors have not those gifts to any extraordinary degree. At best, their work is a mixture of the true and the untrue, which indeed is the case with their betters. None of the masters of fiction has as yet produced a book that is faultless.

With such complexities in mind, it should be evident that the undiscriminating reader who measures the interest and reality of all pieces of fiction by the same standard loses much. He deprives himself of a great deal of pleasure, and he misses experiences of greatest value to his inner life. Unless he distinguishes among the kinds of interest a story may excite, he will find that relatively few tales captivate him at all. He does not know what most of them are about, and he has no taste for them. Those that appeal to him he devours greedily perhaps, but without getting the full flavor of them. He says that they are interesting and real, yet he does not know what he means by either adjective. Soup out of a tin, if hot and strong, will satisfy him as well as the most delicate concoction of the superior cook.

What he really means by interest is that a story gives him a certain mental or nervous excitement —no matter how produced. If the puzzle of plot in a detective story captures his attention, if he can lose track of time and forget himself in the stirring action or amorous adventures of a hero, he says that the tale is interesting, and inquires no further. If the scenes that he reads are vigorously pictured and peppered with a good deal of minor detail, especially if he recognizes the material as similar to something with which he has personal acquaintance—above all, if strong emotions are attributed to the characters that he himself has experienced with lesser force, he declares that the picture of life is real. *Treasure Island* is almost as interesting to him as the stories in the last number of *Adventure*, but not more so. *Tom Jones* is somewhat less real to him than *Anthony Adverse*—for reasons that do him little credit. The feminine counterpart of this unfortunate reader finds as much interest, if she would admit it, in the last serial of the *Woman's Home Companion* as in *Jane Eyre*; as much reality in Miss Willa Cather's delightful romances as in *Vanity Fair*.

There are some readers, furthermore, and equally undiscriminating ones, who never will take a novel seriously unless it conveys information that seems to them valuable, or discusses current ideas, and thus is calculated to have a good influence on minds or morals. The motive of these readers is worthy of respect, but it is far from being a safe guide as to what should be read, and how. They never have observed that a book may be carefully documented, may report with a good deal of accuracy the conditions of the period and the place where the scenes are laid, may be altogether virtuous in purpose, yet be wholly false in human values. In spite of its unessential merits, it may lack the one thing needful. It may indeed be so cheap and devoid of taste as to have a positively evil effect on those who read it.

Let me point out a notorious example of what I mean. Charles Reade's *The Cloister and the Hearth* is still, I am afraid, forced on the attention of boys and girls as a great work of fiction. It is mentioned with respect by historians of literature, who perhaps—let us make the assumption in order to be kind—have not read the book through since they were fifteen. Unquestionably *The Cloister and the Hearth* is informative about the social history of the Renaissance; unquestionably the author intended the book to serve a moral purpose. Vice is punished, and virtue is triumphant in the end. Yet the novel is worthless as a story of human beings and quite unworthy of the repute it has enjoyed. Any reader of adult mind must recognize that the characters have little or no relation to any core of humanity in them. They are puppets merely, to which Reade attributed the power of movement and his own strong feelings. They are not men and women at all. The book, moreover, is no sounder in morals than the average movie out of Hollywood. The wicked are those who oppose the hero, or inconvenience him; the good are those who aid him. Though it has been given to the young as an improving book, it has been read all the years through simply and solely because it is flooded with sentimentalized emotion of the falsest kind. By a curious coincidence, the movement of the screen play was anticipated by this unworthy relic of mid-Victorian England.

As I have said, the demand of readers that fiction be interesting and real is a perfectly legitimate one, nor should we scoff at those who like to have the stories they read informative and stimulating. The difficulty comes in the application of standards that are really fundamental. Undefined and crudely applied, it is evident, they lead only to confusion. Yet they have the validity of most common human judgments if properly understood and controlled. A good story must be, in some way or other, interesting; it must stand in some definite relation to the realities of human life; and it may, without harm to itself, embody useful information or valuable ideas, as well as stir readers to feeling and action. Indeed, some intellectual content and emotional stress it cannot fail to have, else it will not be literature at all.

The point is that the possibilities of variety are so great that the reader, in order to form any reasonable judgment of a story or even to get the full measure of enjoyment from it, must know before taking up a volume, or discover while reading it, what purpose the author had in writing and what end he himself should have in reading. There is no point—indeed, it would be excessively dull of us to do so—in calling Jane Austen dull because her plots are slender. It does not matter that the most violent action in one of her novels is the spraining of an ankle and in another the interruption of some amateur theatricals by an irate father. It is equally unintelligent to suppose that Walter Scott is beneath the attention of the truly intelligent because he failed to develop his characters with the intricate precision of George Eliot or Henry James. A novel, like any other tale in prose or verse, must be read for the qualities it possesses, not for those it does not aim at. In forming our notions of prose fiction it is necessary, then, to distinguish among kinds.

A story—even a very great and noble one—may have no other purpose than to furnish release from the actualities of time and place, or an escape-valve for pent-up emotions. Stories which have this as their chief aim are best called romances, I believe. If we restrict our use of the word romance to this kind of fiction, we shall avoid confusion and do no violence to any established usage. In English the term has gathered a rich connotation of sentiment; we need not care though it has suffered some unjustified opprobrium. It is the happy office of writers of romance to transport their readers—people who may live in humdrum and care-laden ways, as most of us do, or think we do— to the uttermost parts of the sea. Or they take us

out of the present to some past age where life seems
better and more invigorating because strange. Or
they involve us in deeds requiring swift decision,
courage, and inflexible will, where strength of arm
and quickness of brain, together with luck that
often falters but never fails at the last, lead on to
fortune. Or they stir the blood by picturing beings
in whom love is no tepid thing easily frozen by
difficulties, but an overmastering passion—beings
in whom, indeed, all desires and feelings, for good
or for evil, are on an equally grand scale and are
not to be controlled except by honor and possibly
conscience. Sometimes in romance we find a combination of all these appeals, and frequently of
more than one of them.

The reader, whether or not he is conscious of
doing so, participates to some degree in the adventures that are recounted and shares to some
degree the powerful emotions of the characters.
Even though he does not see himself as the hero,
which in childhood we are inclined to do, he enjoys
himself to the extent to which he feels sympa-
thetically with the characters in the story. Reading it is primarily an emotional experience. Since
it has this effect on us, it acts quite inevitably
either as a stimulant or as a narcotic, unless indeed, as sometimes happens, it serves for both. It

is a stimulant in so far as it sets our imagination free to participate in the action and stirs in us the impulse to follow similar adventures. It is a narcotic in that it dulls in us the actualities of our lives and obscures for the time our sense of individual being. We forget ourselves and our normal pursuits quite completely as we read.

It follows, since we tend to live with the figures of the story and to identify ourselves to some extent with one or another of them, that any complete or subtle delineation of character is unnecessary in a romance. The people in fairy-tales, for example, which belong in this category, are always simple. They are scarcely individuals at all. The wicked stepmothers are wicked stepmothers and nothing more, the young adventurers are merely young men to whom extraordinary things happen, the beautiful princesses have no qualities except beauty and kindness. Although these creatures in folk-tales often go about in disguise or suffer marvellous transformations, they remain thin and almost symbolic figures. Similarly the romances in verse and prose, which in varying forms furnished the chief mental relaxation of readers and auditors from the twelfth century to the eighteenth, seldom showed character related to action. They had no need to do so, for the men and women in these

stories were there only to have adventures through
which readers or hearers might enter a world of
make-believe and fulfilled desire. Human moods
often were delicately and subtly conveyed in the
old romances, and human aspirations, loves, and
hates were shown, but not individualized characters except in rare instances.

Later, makers of picaresque tales discovered
that sharply defined rogues and vagabonds gave
zest to the kind of romance they were writing and
drew them accordingly. Still later, Scott by his
wizardry taught the world how to combine the
virtues of the novel with the pleasures of romance
—an achievement for which he has not received
even yet all the credit due him. Because of his
example many romances have been written during
the past century which contain portraits of solidly
imagined human beings. Yet it remains true that
we read, and ought to read, such stories without
demanding of them such representation and analysis of individuals as is proper to the novel.
Treasure Island is a better book, a richer book,
because Long John Silver plays his part in it; but
the appeal he makes is only subsidiary, after all, to
Stevenson's main purpose, which was to show the
achievement of a mysterious and difficult quest for
treasure. The other characters of the story, you

will recall, are thinly sketched. They are adequate, but they raise none of the questions that Long John stirs within us.

It is important to understand that romances may equally well be plausible or wholly impossible of belief as transcripts of events occurring on our planet. The material and the treatment of it may be poles apart in this respect. Defoe made *Robinson Crusoe* so credible that the citizens of London, unaccustomed to reading fiction and suspicious of such things, could feel themselves having all the experiences, factual and spiritual, that the hero underwent. It was the romance of common sense. Defoe compelled the belief of his first audience, as he still makes us accept his matter-of-fact statements that on this day Robinson laid out a plantation and on that saw the footprint in the sands. At the other extreme, William Beckford in *Vathek* and Mary Shelley in *Frankenstein* did not try to make their parables credible as real adventures, any more than did Samuel Johnson his very different parable called *Rasselas*. There is no pretence in such cases that the events narrated ever took place. *Vathek* and *Frankenstein* are romances of fantasy and terror, *Rasselas* of disillusioned reason, but they belong in the same category with *Robinson Crusoe*. None of the books can be enjoyed properly or judged aright if it be read as a novel is read.

Place side by side two such charming tales of young love as *Aucassin and Nicolette* and Thomas Hardy's *Under the Greenwood Tree*. The *cantefable* from the thirteenth century is woven of fantastic adventures, adventures so fantastic that the unknown author did not even try to keep a straight face while recounting some of them. Aucassin's capture of the Count of Bougars is a bit of intentional humor, while the habits of the King of Torelore are treated as broad farce. Hardy's story, on the other hand, moves from one homely event to another in a corner of England which the author had known since boyhood. Yet the two are alike in their essential quality. What interests us—the matter of real importance—is not the personalities of the lovers but love itself, a sweet and unspoiled passion, growing up and surmounting obstacles until it reaches a happy consummation.

These romances that I have been mentioning, whether credible or incredible, are not untrue to life. Some of them, like *Rasselas*, are perhaps almost unduly instructive about the nature of life. They do not reveal, however, the secrets of human personality. For the most part, they furnish the reader some kind of emotional release. They are the spirit and substance of adventure and desire. Human moods are exemplified in them, often with great justice and power, but not—except to give them a subsidiary appeal, as in *Treasure Island*—human characters. Romances are free in a world of fancy, and they set us free. There is no reason why we should condescend to them. They will be written and read as long as there is blood in man's veins and impulse moves him.

A great deal of fiction, however, is sharply distinguished from this kind. There are stories, the main object of which is to represent and interpret human beings as individuals, and by this means to furnish the reader with vicarious experience of life itself. How people behave, why they behave as they do, how they think, how they feel, what they are like altogether: these are the staples of such books, which in English we call novels. They attract us peculiarly because men and women are, after all, the most interesting phenomena on the planet. Pope's statement about the proper study of mankind has the virtue of many such truisms— it is profoundly true. The individual's experience is necessarily limited, but it may be widened to an indefinite degree, and deepened as well, by reading what men of acute mind have recorded about other men. Biography furnishes him with this vicarious experience, but not in the same way and not at all with the same freedom as fiction. A biography is confined to the study of a single individual, whereas fiction, whether in the form of drama or of narrative, can represent an individual who not only is himself but sums up characteristics common to many individuals. Sometimes he is the epitome of a great body of human beings. He can be both particular and universal.

Imagination—about the operations of which we are still so ignorant—somehow enables the exceptionally gifted artist to distill by obscure intuitive processes from his observation and experience much truth about the mind and heart of man. This knowledge finds embodiment in the characters round whom he weaves his story. The reader or the play-goer may freely share in the author's store of wisdom up to the point of his own capacity to receive it. He has the opportunity to do so, that is. He will not get as much as he should if he depends on idle absorption, but by attention he can learn more than a little.

Stories of the sort I have been sketching are no new thing in literature of course. They existed long before the modern novel was conceived. Certain epics, for example, have the qualities that are in question. The wanderings of Odysseus form a tale of adventure, but Odysseus emerges from it at the end a humanized figure, solid and understandable —no mere puppet of the gods, or of Homer. Other poets than the makers of epics, too, have had the same purpose, and have known how to interpret mankind by creating significant individuals who act in accordance with their natures. Chaucer did this with a mastery that few writers in any medium have equalled. Many of the Canterbury pilgrims, as well as the immortal trio in *Troilus and Criseyde*, bear witness to his power. Three hundred and fifty years before his time, moreover, a lady of the Japanese court had written in prose the marvellous *Tale of Genji*, which pictured the people of her day with such compelling art that in spite of their strange ways of thought and action they live for us even yet. Before the year 1022 the Lady Murasaki had achieved one of the great novels of the world. At the beginning of the seventeenth century another genius, this time a man, wrote a very different book which has the same quality of picturing individuals who are themselves as well as significant representatives of the human race. Don Quixote and Sancho Panza not only embody certain traits that are universal, but are persons who have individual being quite as we do.

In the course of the eighteenth century the habit of writing fiction with emphasis on character, and action shaped by character, became at length very common. The history of the modern novel had begun. For about two hundred years authors have been trying, with greater or less success, to tell us through novels what they have learned about life and the people who inhabit the globe. They have experimented in numberless ways, for it became evident at once that the art of the novel could not be reduced to a formula. Wise critics never have attempted to lay down any set of rules for it. The novel has been a very various thing, responsive to changing tastes, to changed conditions, and above all to the personal qualities of each man and woman of independent talent who has written stories of the kind. It has remained constant only in the predominance given to character shown in action.

Fielding wrote an orderly novel, and Laurence Sterne one that defied all order. Thackeray took Vanity Fair for his scene and Balzac an even larger field, while Jane Austen wrote with equal success about a little group of provincial gentlefolk. Scott romanticized in the grand style, and Dickens romanticized in a wholly different way. Hawthorne and Melville, though contemporaries, have little in common. The work of Arnold Bennett does not much resemble that of Joseph Conrad. Material and method have altered from individual to individual and from decade to decade, but the novel has remained. Dire prophecies of its extinction, too boldly uttered, have come to naught as new writers have found new ways to interpret our fellows to us and us to ourselves.

Because novels have this instructive quality, because we can and do acquire some human wisdom from them, it does not follow that we find them less captivating than tales focused on action. The interest is different, that is all. The plot may be quite as exciting, indeed, and the emotional pitch quite as high as in any romance, but the feelings stirred in us will be deeper, since the things that happen in the story concern beings whom we recognize as individuals like ourselves. We say of them that they are "real," and are correspondingly moved by their enjoyments and their sufferings. There is a causal relation, too, between what they are and what they endure—a rough approach, at least, to the logic of events, which gives us satisfaction in that it seems to warrant our emotion.

What adventure, after all, can be so exciting as the adventure in which the destiny of a human being whom we have come to know intimately is decided? There is an authenticity about the experiences of Richard Feverel, of Kim, of Tom Jones, of Maggie Tulliver, of Jane Eyre, which affects us with peculiar force. We learn not only what they do but what they are, and our deeper sympathies are stirred accordingly. As they come to knowledge of themselves and of the world, we to some extent advance in wisdom. However little we profit by the vicarious adventure—and the degree to which we do so, as I have said, depends upon ourselves—we have been close spectators of it, and we have been given the opportunity to understand the significance of it.

The novelist has at his command, it must not be forgotten, all the resources of the writer of romance. Conrad takes us to the China Seas, though Jane Austen only to Bath. Dickens furnishes us with melodrama as well as poignant tragedy and extravagant humor. Thomas Hardy, like Dostoevsky, heightens his dramatic appeal by the atmosphere in which he bathes his stories. The novel is not properly a dissection of human beings but an attempt to picture them as they are and to interpret them. All the wonder of the world may be in it.

As we shall see later, there is no point in attempting to establish a hierarchy of values in fiction too precisely, or to say whether one kind is greater and another kind less great. Each must be read and enjoyed and judged for what it is. Legitimate pleasure may be got from the tale that releases the fancy or that induces in us an heroic or a tranquil mood. Legitimate pleasure may be got from the tale that permits us to know men and women beyond our personal experience, and more fully than we know even our close kinsfolk and friends. There is profit, too, as well as pleasure, in both kinds of fiction. The profit and the pleasure may even be found together in a single story. The book of which we should beware is that in which the author pretends to furnish us one kind of entertainment while really foisting off on us another. False values are as dangerous in fiction as in any other art. It is only a verbal paradox—not a real paradox at all—to say that all fiction should be true. Our next business, then, should be to examine what we mean when we assert that a story is real or is not real.

(2)

The Real and the Unreal in Fiction

OF the various terms which gained currency among literary critics in the nineteenth century none has done more to befog clarity of understanding than the word realism. Whatever may have been its value to the criticism of painting, it has been an unmitigated nuisance when applied to fiction. I have said already that the undiscriminating reader frequently calls a story real for no other reason than that the scenes are vigorously pictured and amply detailed, or—even oftener—because the emotions attributed to the characters are served hot from the griddle. So much has the word been misused, indeed, that such a reader has a tendency to call any novel he likes realistic, no matter what its content and manner; or, on the other hand, he may call it realistic because the material is sordid and unpleasant to his taste. Nor can the common reader be blamed for the muddle he is in. If he reads book reviews at all, he finds at every turn the same loose and meaningless use of "realism" and "realistic." If he has studied works of fiction in school or college, he has heard his teachers fall back on the words, sometimes by way of commendation and sometimes of blame. Teachers, like other critics, have been misled, on the one hand, by failing to analyze with sufficient care the impressions they have received and, on the other, by supposing the intentions of authors to be a safe guide to what they really have achieved.

Let us look at the latter difficulty first of all. Every honest novelist believes himself to be setting down a true picture of life. He wishes to show things and people, and the things people do, quite as they are. They are clear to his imagination, or at least they seem to him so at the time when he is composing. He tries his best to write what he sees. If life is to him a great and terrible thing, he tries to show it as great and terrible. If life is a grubby thing, he tries to show it as grubby. He must be honest with himself and with his audience. In these latter times, therefore, since the day when the term was popularized, he cannot very well avoid thinking of himself as a "realist" unless indeed he adopts some other epithet to mark his integrity of purpose. Yet what he sets down is so colored by his way of looking at the world that it bears little or no resemblance to the work of another novelist who likewise believes himself to be a realist. This may be so even when their raw material is pretty much the same. In a word, there is no point in his use of the term. Furthermore, critics will be found to deny hotly that novelist A is a realist at all, whereas they will defend with equal ardor the realism of novelist B. Other critics will reverse the use of the word: to them A is a realist, and B most decidedly is not.

Again, the failure to analyze carefully the impression made by a novel has led all too often to a use of "realism" and "realistic" absurd in itself and indicative at the same time of the futile vagueness of the terms. The critic, like the common reader, has felt himself, for example, moved by a piece of fiction and has recognized a certain power in it. Also he has observed that the scenes are pictured with an abundance of what we may call corroborative detail. The appearances, the dress, the movements of the characters, their surroundings and their way of living, have been shown with a great deal of circumstance. Accordingly he describes the book as realistic. Yet the characters themselves and everything they are supposed to think, to do, and to say may be wholly false. If scrutinized with attention, they may be found to be inconsistently drawn, with thoughts and actions attributed to them that make no sense. The reader may be moved only because of the strong, though possibly quite absurd, emotional stresses with which the author has emphasized the imagined situations. In other words, the story may be utterly worthless. To call such a novel realistic is folly, yet month by month and year by year the folly is committed by lazy-minded critics who will not take the trouble to analyze what they read.

Through a similar lack of reasonably careful thought most novels that picture the life of the very poor and the oppressive conditions of industrial and agricultural labor are classed, quite without regard to their inherent qualities, as realistic. At the moment such books are known, to be sure, as "proletarian"—a term even emptier of meaning as it is used; but they are believed to be realistic, one and all. Yet an examination of them will show that they treat reality in a great variety of ways and cannot properly be placed in a unified group. In the same way, emphasis on a definite regional background for a story is supposed to make it realistic, though a little reflection will disclose the wide differences of approach and method found in such fiction, which may quite well be lovely and satisfying romance rather than a study in the realities of human character. *Tobacco Road* is not romance, certainly, but most of the nostalgic fiction of the South is nothing else.

"Realism" and "realistic," it must be clear to any thoughtful person, are not only quite inexact terms in themselves, but have been so misused that any value they might have had has vanished long since. They are a nuisance, as I have said. We shall do well to forget them. Yet the need remains of some means by which to appraise the attitude towards reality assumed by the creator of any work of fiction. All stories, we agree, have a definite relationship to reality. What we must get at, if we can, is an understanding of this relationship in the particular case. Unless we do so, we are liable to strange errors in judging the worth of a story and, not improbably, to a failure in enjoying it as it ought to be enjoyed.

Let us clear our minds, to begin with, of any notion that fiction is, or ever can be, a copy of life. A story is composed of words, and words are a very small part of life, though an important one. You can show what people and things are like by the use of words; you can convey to another your impression of them and your considered estimate of them; but you cannot reproduce them. Things and people have solid substance, whereas language is a conventionalized means of communication through the medium of sound, which in books is recorded by a series of symbols. Even history can at best be only a representation of events that the historian has reason to believe have occurred, together with his interpretation of them. History cannot reproduce what has happened. Fiction is at least one degree further removed from actuality. In fiction, for the most part, both the events and the people are imagined and have only counterparts, not prototypes, in the physical world. Conversation is the only element of a story that even belongs to the same category of existence as what is represented. The author makes the characters in his novel talk somewhat as people talk in real life, though—fortunately for the reader—he does not try to give full reports of the imagined conversations. They are digests rather than stenographic records, and of course digests of talks that might have taken place, not of interchanges that have been made at some time or other by creatures in the flesh.

Apart from talk, then, a work of fiction is in no respect a reproduction of life, or a slice of life; it merely tells us about imagined people and the imagined events in which they have a part. The notion popularized in the last century by Emile Zola that a novel could be a document for the scientific study of social history and psychology was one of the absurdest ever concocted by perverse criticism. Only a world somewhat intoxicated by recent successes in investigating the phenomena of existence could have taken it seriously. Yet even to-day the idea persists that a novel may be a copy of life, if not precisely a reproduction, and that its worth depends on the fidelity with which mundane events are depicted with dimensional accuracy.

Readers and critics, when they say that a book is true to life usually have in mind—if very vaguely —a dimensional accuracy of this sort, with the dimensions measured by their own senses. They are the better pleased if they hear that the author has known someone even remotely resembling this character or that, for the supposition of a model gives them confidence in the portraiture. They distrust what imagination can do, distrust its power in what we loosely call creation, but hold a pathetic belief in the capacity of authors to observe with photographic accuracy, though they must know that all testimony based on human observation is notoriously fallible.

It is a curious fact that, in spite of the notions to which I have just referred, the average reader does not let his love for what I have called dimensional accuracy, and his belief in the possibility of the crude transference of observation to fiction, control his taste. He pays lip-service to the idea of what he calls realism; he finds an interest in measuring an author's observation by his own; but he is captivated by the story that beguiles him or stirs his feelings. He is not to be condemned for so doing. Fiction ought, by one means or another, to capture the sympathetic interest of him who reads. Only we ought, as readers, to be aware of the means, and call things by their right names. We ought to enjoy a romance as a romance, a novel as a novel; and we shall very greatly widen our capacity for enjoyment, as well as intensify it, if we think clearly about the stories we read.

To this end it is of fundamental importance, as I was saying, that we come to a clear understanding about reality in fiction, to learn what the nature of it is and whether it is an unvarying quality.

Perhaps the matter can be best approached by trying to see whether in practice all authors assume, and expect their readers to assume, the same attitude towards the reality they are trying with equally honest purpose to represent. Since they cannot reproduce life, as we have seen, but only describe and suggest it, they must of necessity conventionalize, using symbols or images, using indeed a whole battery of rhetorical and schematic devices with which the story-telling tradition of the race has provided them. The question really comes down to this: Do they conventionalize in the same way? Do they even try to picture reality by the same means? Is the reality shown by Fielding and Hardy, Jane Austen and Mrs. Gaskell, Stendhal and Thackeray, Turgenieff and Dickens all one in its method of representation? Obviously not, yet the men and women named have somehow so managed to interpret life to us that we acknowledge their mastery. Somehow what they have written is, we say, true to life. Yet if so, it is not true to life in the same fashion. They composed their novels with different attitudes towards men and things, and used different methods of representation, which we as readers accept. To refuse this acceptance is to deny the validity of the author's interpretation of the world, which one is free to do, but ought not to do—in the case of an artist who has had a great following of intelligent readers for a long time—without a careful examination. Dickens furnishes an instance in point. It is unwise to say jauntily that his portraits lack reality until we make sure what we mean by reality and how

Dickens was trying to picture reality. The fact that Mr. Pickwick and Alfred Jingle live in the memory of the world as they do, a hundred years after their creation, should give us pause if we are tempted to say that such strange beings are not, after all, human.

Doubtless it is true that there are almost as many ways of looking at life and of picturing men and things as there have been, and will be, writers with original and really creative imaginations. We can, however, group these individual attitudes in a set of useful categories. We can establish, that is, various planes of reality, as we may call them, upon which events and characters are customarily presented in fiction. By observing these planes of reality, I believe, we shall be able to get a better understanding of what is true in romances and novels and perhaps a clearer notion of what is false. Upon all the planes truth may be expressed, reality may be justly represented, human events and human beings may be presented. Upon all of them likewise an author's observation and imagination may go astray, and he may write fiction that has no significance, or—worse than that— fiction that wholly misinterprets the stuff of life.

There is, first of all, the plane of actuality. A story pretends to be a record of events that have happened to people for whom birth-certificates could at need be produced, and in places that ought to be found on maps—even though they do not appear on those we have at command. Such a story apes biography, or chronicle, or history. The writer seems to be trying to induce the belief that he is not a maker of fiction at all, and sometimes he employs every artifice at his command to produce an illusion of reality, or, one might say, an illusion of actuality. Daniel Defoe, who had a masterly hand at this kind of thing, succeeded in attracting to his stories of adventure and crime a puritanical audience for whom pleasure had to be veiled by a cloak of mental and moral instruction. Though well aware that Robinson Crusoe and Captain Singleton and Moll Flanders were invented characters, they could take them as real and their adventures as true tales. Defoe's manner was so sober, the circumstantial detail out of which he wove his fabric so credible, that wild romance appeared in the garb of acceptable autobiography. Nor has the effectiveness of it gone after more than two centuries. We still can be cajoled into a suspension of unbelief by Crusoe's plain narrative.

Nor is Defoe the only writer of romances who has taken pains to keep his tales on the plane of actuality. A long line of authors, purveyors of adventure and mystery, from Defoe's day to our own, have seen that the immediate credibility to be attained by the pretence of making a plain record of actual happenings has its value for such fiction. A good deal of Stevenson's effectiveness as a spinner of yarns came from his carefulness in this respect. He forces us very often to accept wildly improbable events by depicting them with the sobriety of a dispassionate observer and with an abundance of sharply visualized detail. Mr. John Buchan has shown—and one hopes that Lord Tweedsmuir will continue to show—much the same gift in our own time. Surprising and delightful adventures are recounted in *Prester John* and *Huntingtower*, but nothing that might not have happened, we are led to believe, at the times and in the places where the scenes are laid. The illusion of reality is maintained throughout. The same thing is true of the better specimens of the vast crop of detective fiction which has been harvested during the last generation. The avid reader knows quite as well as the author that the crimes described and the intricate ways by which the evil-doers are discovered are purely fictitious, yet reader and author agree to look upon them as real events. This conspiracy is necessary, since, if the pretence of actuality were for a moment forgotten, the whole narrative would be pointless. Curiously enough, the fact that the mystery story is one of the most artificial forms of fiction, and appeals to us as an intellectual problem, does not affect the manner of its telling.

In most such tales of mystery, it is important to observe, as well as in most romances of adventure, the personalities of the characters involved count for very little. Defoe's heroes and heroines, for example, are mere projections of the author; and the detectives of fiction are usually embodied habits, mental and physical. They need be nothing more, for the action is what matters: action kept evenly on the plane of actuality.

In the novel, where the emphasis of the story is primarily on character, and action shaped by character, the state of things is very different. A little observation shows that the novelists have been far less careful than the writers of adventure and mystery stories to pretend that their fiction is anything else than fiction. It is necessary, or at least useful, for the latter to keep to the plane of actuality, but it is not at all important for the interpreter of character to do so. More often than not, the great novelists have made no effort whatever to capture and preserve in their work such an illusion of reality as we have been considering.

Richardson somewhat bunglingly attempted it by the futile device of telling his stories by means of letters, but his achievement lay in quite other directions. Jane Austen, perfecting a technique in which she had predecessors but was destined to have no rivals, kept her novels wholly within the plane of actuality. Although she made no protestations of fidelity to fact, her tales come closer to being representations of the world as it would have been seen and understood by a member of the circle described than does the work of almost any other English novelist. In other words, her people might well have lived where and when they are shown as living, might have thought and said and done what they are represented as thinking, saying, and doing.

It is instructive to observe why this should have been the case. Miss Austen took her material from a very restricted field of human kind and social background. There are no conspicuous figures in any walk of life among her characters. Consequently she could handle them quite as if they had lived in the flesh. Their verisimilitude, the sense of actuality they convey, is furthermore increased by the author's willingness to let them interpret themselves to the reader in speech and action with very little comment on her part. This last-mentioned advantage was sacrificed by another great novelist, George Eliot, who guided her readers with extremest care to an understanding of her characters, but nevertheless kept them on the plane of actuality. Like Miss Austen, she assumed their veritable existence. Flaubert, in *Madame Bovary*, did very much the same thing, as did Turgenieff in his characteristic work.

Most novelists, however, as I have said, have not tried to keep to this plane, which does not mean at all that they have been less truthful in their representations of life. Many of them, and among these some of the greatest, have adopted the second attitude to which I wish to call attention. They have pictured human beings on what we may call a plane of imagined reality. They make no pretence that their characters are not fictional and the events of a story wholly in the realm of imagination. Yet this realm is as close a counterpart of the world in which we live as the author can make it, and the inhabitants correspond in every way to the men and women of our world.

Henry Fielding furnishes as good an example of this procedure as one could wish to find. Because he did not pretend that his comic prose epic, as he called it, was a record of actual happenings, he gave people names like Allworthy, to express approbation, like Square and Thwackum, to show his scorn of those gentlemen; he invented fictitious places and yet used also real places like the inn at Upton; he made no attempt at credibility, in short, if credibility be a matter of perfect illusion. Who can deny, nevertheless, that *The History of Tom Jones* is as truthful, as just, as real a picture of life as ever has been set down? In their different ways Thackeray and Balzac created imaginary worlds somewhat as Fielding did, but peopled them far more densely. Thackeray's conception of Vanity Fair, which extended throughout his later novels, forced him, it is reasonable to say, from the plane of actuality to the plane of imagined reality. That he used Oxbridge for Oxford and used punning names for some of his characters is not a matter of great moment, though an indication of his attitude. Of more importance is the fact that his imagination would have been shackled if he had pretended to be writing anything else than fiction. His books would have lost rather than gained verisimilitude, if he had not been free to invent an aristocracy for the acquaintance of Major Pendennis, and a wide circle of varying elements, within which to display Becky Sharp. The same thing is true of Balzac: his *comédie humaine* is far more real than it could have been, if he had not imagined a counterpart of the world he knew, and given his characters their being within it. This counterfeit world has plenty of correspondences with the world of actuality, but is independent of it—something that Balzac created. Trollope worked in the same tradition, building up with patient industry and steady imagination a replica of Victorian England, which is quite as real as the England described by the historians and in many respects more comprehensible. Arnold Bennett, who seems to me the most important of the British and American novelists in the generation just passing, dealt in the same way with reality. Like many of his great predecessors, he represented men and women with singular fidelity but did not scruple to treat his characters as imaginary beings.

There have been other eminent novelists, again, about whom the most significant thing in respect of their attitude to reality is the marked heightening of emphasis with which they have shown it: a heightening so very marked in many cases that they have been accused of not representing life at all. Yet sober analysis will show, I believe, that some of the authors so accused have given us interpretations of men and women that rank among the most penetrating that have appeared in fiction. They have worked on what we may term the plane of heightened reality, that is all. That they have been peculiarly subject to false valuations, sometimes to extravagant praise for the wrong reasons and sometimes to quite undeserved blame, is because readers and critics have persisted in applying to their work the test of dimensional accuracy to which I referred on an earlier page. Their novels, it is true, do not keep to dimensional accuracy. Characters are distorted, emotions and desires are pushed beyond the point of credibility, events are manipulated, for the sake of effect, without much regard to verisimilitude. Realities of human character and human destiny may, nevertheless, be communicated in them quite as justly as in fiction that keeps more accurately the proportion of things. The power of observation, the intuitional acuteness, the human wisdom of such novelists cannot be denied. They give us magnified or whimsical or distorted or highly emotionalized views of life, but the truth notwithstanding.

In other respects than this matter of heightened reality they do not constitute a unified group at all. When I name Dickens, Scott, Thomas Hardy, the Bronte sisters, and Melville, it will be seen how widely they differ from one another in material and method. Yet I feel sure that it is profitable for us to look at the authors mentioned with reference to this one point. I have chosen them, indeed, partly because they are so divergent in every other respect. They illustrate how variously fiction may be affected by heightening the plane of reality on which the imagined characters are shown.

Scott, it scarcely need be said, tended to magnify everything he treated. He himself, acutest in self-criticism among all our novelists as he was, referred to the big bow-wow strain in his work. There was justice in this, as well as an undue degree of self-disparagement. He drew his characters along simple lines, throwing into sharp relief both their vices and their virtues, and correspondingly making their joys and sorrows and perplexities appear somewhat greater than do those of common men. These figures, so conceived and executed, move among events imagined equally on a grand scale. I do not mean that some of the best portraits are not those of humble folk and some of the best scenes homely in their settings and quiet of mood. Even these, however, Sir Walter touched with his wand of magic, transforming into greatness what might have seemed very ordinary if otherwise treated. His novels, though they have many faults, are done in the grand manner and on a scale of amplitude still unrivalled. No one has shown with greater power and justice the deep springs of human action, which is why we can be sure that reality is revealed in his work. The reality is heightened, that is all.

In a wholly different way Dickens was unable to picture life with dimensional accuracy. For him the outlines of people and the course of events were distorted by humor, by intense feeling, by the sharpness of his vision, by the violence of his whole nature. Instinctively he caricatured everything, and he developed his magnificent artistry on the foundation-stones of caricature. He has been accused, sometimes by those professing to be admirers, of not picturing human beings at all, but a race apart only roughly corresponding to the inhabitants of earth. Yet one only has to read his novels to become aware that his powers of observation were singularly acute. He had looked keenly on the phenomena of life and had stored up impressions of them more richly than have most other great novelists. These impressions became distorted by his imagination, it is true, but in such a way that the qualities of the men and women he created stood out with unmistakable clarity. Never are we at a loss to understand his conception or his judgment of a character, as we sometimes are with Thackeray's people, for example. The figures he drew come to life through their actions, moreover, seeming more and more human as we gain greater familiarity with them. Even though they move among events which are strangely distorted also, in an odd world of exaggerated sentiment and Gothic violence, they have being—they live. They are representations of reality, but of reality shown in caricature.

Charlotte Bronte illustrates in still another way how reality may be heightened without the sacrifice of truth. When she wrote *Jane Eyre*, she had a very limited experience of life, and she was not gifted with unusual powers of observation. These deficiencies she supplied to some extent from her reading of fiction, but of fiction not always of the most faithful sort, though emotionally vigorous. With this equipment, it would not have seemed likely that she could write a novel of importance. Fortunately she had the intuition of genius, emotional intensity of a rare order, a native gift for narrative technique almost as astonishing as Miss Austen's, and a command of style that she had developed by practice in writing throughout her girlhood. By letting her heroine tell the story, she made a virtue of her own defects and produced one of the great masterpieces of English fiction. The characters and the events are shown as Jane

Eyre came to know them, colored by her prejudices, intensified by her violent emotions, yet steadied by her sober sanity: all of which emanated from Miss Bronte herself. The areas of ignorance she exposed do not matter, since the intuitive perception and the intensity of feeling give both depth and elevation to the story. It is a magnificent recording of life, though of life heightened beyond ordinary conceptions of reality. That *Shirley* is less good than *Jane Eyre* and *Villette* resulted from Miss Bronte's attempt to conform to more customary habits of novel-writing, which were unsuitable to the amplest display of her gifts.

Emily Bronte presents an even more extreme case than her sister of essentially the same heightening. Less experienced and disciplined by contact with the world, lacking the vein of hard common sense that Charlotte possessed, she had an amazing insight into the elemental passions that control human action. These she showed in operation, with a power that owed much to her gift of seeing everything within her vision in the sharpest of images— the gift that made her also a poet of distinction. Neither Heathcliff nor Catherine is a synthesized human being, but they are eternally and tragically true as embodiments of love and hate. The tiresome gabble about the relative merit of the two

Brontes, which has gone on intermittently ever since they wrote, would be silenced, I believe, if their essential qualities were understood. Each was a genius in her own right, and each therefore differed from the other. They differed even in the thing they shared: their power of communicating with white-hot intensity what they had learned by intuition about the human heart.

Thomas Hardy is another writer whose work cannot be justly estimated unless one recognizes that his characters and scenes are conceived and executed on a plane of heightened reality rather than in accordance with nature as nature is ordinarily observed. No one has been less coolly objective in the representation of life. Because he laid his novels in a definitely fixed quarter of England, with descriptions of easily identifiable places slightly masked by fictitious names, and because he recorded with careful fidelity the folkways of the people living in the region, the objectionable word "realist" has been applied to him. Nothing could be more inexact. When we observe how he used coincidence to bring to pass the evils decreed by fate, how he forced upon characters actions quite out of keeping with the qualities with which he had endowed them, as is the case, for example, both in *The Return of the Native* and *Tess*, we realize that his virtues as a novelist are not those of an author who saw life steadily and saw it whole. Rather, he saw and pictured it with heightened emotions, which in themselves were just as well as powerful. Real tragedy he could not write, but as melodrama his work is magnificent. He must be placed among our greatest novelists, but among those whose sense of reality was controlled by feeling instead of clear perception.

Herman Melville is interesting in this connection because he combined in so unusual a way the exactest use of detail with extreme emotional heightening in his treatment of character and of situation. Although he had a sense of tragedy far profounder and far more just than that by which Hardy was ridden, he had certain important qualities in common with him. The beauty of the South Sea idylls and the power of *Moby Dick* cannot be appreciated unless we observe that all his work was done on the plane of heightened reality.

We come at last to a fourth category of writers in respect of their attitude towards the real world. There have been—and doubtless the kind will continue to appear—a good many novelists whose imaginations have exercised a certain filtration of qualities in representing human kind, with the result that their men and women appear less solidly embodied than are the creations of other authors, though subtly drawn and often of the highest interpretative value. Such novelists may be said to work on a plane of selective reality. Selection takes place, to be sure, in all imaginative work, but it operates in a special way with the authors whom I have in mind. It is a matter quite as much of seeing, I believe, as of representation. Only those attributes of character that have significance for the purposes of the story develop in the writer's imagination as he creates, and therefore only such attributes are shown. Events and places appear with normal outline and substance: the human beings are the one element of the fiction affected by the imaginative filtration, as I have called it.

Perhaps Nathaniel Hawthorne illustrates what I mean more clearly than anyone else. Time and again, he has been accused by his critics of representing not the substance of life but a world of shadows. No one has arisen to deny his talent altogether, but there has been rather insistent complaint that his people are not real, either as New Englanders or as citizens of any other country. They are not real, indeed, if judged by the criteria that are applicable to Miss Austen or Thackeray. But the fault lies with the critics, who have been singularly blind to the nature of Hawthorne's accomplishment. If the reader will observe the characters in *The Scarlet Letter* or *The House of Seven Gables*, he will see that Hawthorne endows them with those qualities only which will serve to illuminate and interpret the moral problems with which they are involved. What we find is a highly selective representation of human traits, but one that is very just as far as it goes. We learn what we need to know about Arthur Dimmesdale, for instance, and we get it powerfully focused because nowhere obscured by unessentials. Viewed in this way, Hawthorne's work shows for what it is: a wonderfully penetrating criticism of life.

Somewhat the same thing is true, I believe, of Henry James, who—whether he knew it or not—began as a disciple of Hawthorne. A certain thinness in his representation of characters always has left a good many readers, who have not known how to take him, with a sense of dissatisfaction. In spite of the subtle and—in his older years—prolix examination to which he subjected his people, in spite of the rich variety with which he showed their reactions to the problems of their lives, he represented only those traits that were pertinent to those problems. In its own way and directed to its own ends, his imagination was as selective as Hawthorne's. He secured a unity of impression thereby, as well as subtlety, but of course he did not draw full-blooded, full-bodied men and women.

After another fashion Meredith furnishes a good example of the procedure we are considering. Although the effervescence of his wit, his restless energy, and the rich emotional life with which he endowed his characters gave his work a quality very different from anything in Hawthorne or James, he was like them in the way he conceived and drew the human figures who illustrate the ideas that run throughout his novels. Consider so famous a person as Sir Willoughby Patterne. What do we know of him, after all, except that he was a rich and handsome egotist? Meredith so completely focused his own attention and ours on the one all-encompassing vice that we get the other attributes of Sir Willoughby only by implication. The method suffices. We have no doubt of his reality, and we are shaken by the spectacle; but we never get the sort of acquaintance with him that we have, for instance, with the people whom George Eliot drew. Meredith's characters flash upon us briefly, or are shown in a multitude of flashes until their deepest secrets are fully exposed, yet they never appear except in a filtered light which reveals only those things that the author thought it expedient for us to see.

What interested Joseph Conrad, apart from the vicissitudes of human adventure, were the states of mind in which men encountered the crises that came upon them. Like James, he was more intent than was Hawthorne on the mental and spiritual phenomena that accompanied a conflict, but he had a keener sense than James for the dramatic moment. Hence he produced something new in fiction: yarns of adventure, seldom well ordered, in which the consciousness of at least one figure is shown with extraordinary elaboration. The result would have been incoherence if he had not viewed people with an eye that registered only such attributes as were relevant to the moral crisis that lay at the heart of the story. The plane of selective reality was the only one on which he could have worked with success, and we should read him with this in mind.

I would not have it thought that I regard the categories which I have been discussing as fixed or inflexible. Differences of judgment there may well be as to the classification of some of the novelists I have mentioned. Very possibly one and another of them may belong in more than one group, for the artist's attitude to his material need not be unvarying. I am persuaded, however, that unless we are aware of more than one possible approach to reality in fiction, we lose much pleasure and are liable to gross misunderstanding. In reading an author we ought to try at least to see the world as he saw it. To be more than the pursuit of an idle hour, fiction must somehow or other have the truth of life in it; but there is no reason why the representation of life should conform to a single standard. The world of man is so complex that reality may be expressed in widely different ways. The wise reader is he who discriminates among them but is appreciative of sound work, however done. He will not confuse the view of things taken by Marcel Proust with that of Walter Scott, and he ought not to be content to evade thought by using borrowed terms like "realism" and "idealism," which hinder rather than help our understanding.

(3)

Form in Fiction

OF all things made by the art of man fiction
is least subject to inevitable laws or conventions. The nine-and-sixty ways of narrative—every
one of them right—to which Kipling once referred,
do not exhaust the possibilities. Most responsive
to the will of the author, the material of stories
may be so envisaged and manipulated as to bear
the stamp of his personality, no matter how sensible or how wrong-headed he may be. A story may
begin anywhere, tell much or little, stress character
or action or setting, each virtually to the exclusion
of the other elements. It may be so framed as to
seem the record of events that have happened at a
real place at a specified time, or it may be pure
fantasy. It may be simple in theme or extremely
complex. It may picture the surfaces of life or
present a subtly made analysis of what goes on
within the minds of people. The range from which

the material of it may come is as wide as earth, as high as heaven, as deep as hell.

With a scope like this, and with a fluidity in treatment that makes anything possible, doubting Thomas is justified in asking whether there can be form in fiction at all: whether there is any use in discussing the matter. If any imaginable device can be right in a particular case, he may say, is it not futile to talk about design? Doubting Thomas has to be answered. We also have to admit the correctness of his premise. The story-teller, whatever be his medium, certainly may use, and ought to use, the method, the manner, the design—or the apparent lack of one—that will make his tale most effective. The widest latitude of treatment is permitted the author.

Yet two things may persuade us that the domain of narrative is not a complete anarchy. In the first place, we know all too well that stories may be very dull. We have suffered the unspeakable boredom of the listener on whose ears beat waves of unessential detail from the lips of a man or woman who can begin, but cannot soon conclude, the recital of some insignificant happening. In private audience or public speech such catastrophes occur. The listener cannot escape, and he knows that the anecdote, if told at all, should be told another way.

The raconteur's method is not one of the permissible nine-and-sixty. It is equally true that written fiction may bore us. Sometimes we may be bored, as I have indicated earlier, through some fault in ourselves; but not infrequently it comes about through some kind of ineptitude on the part of the author.

We begin a novel, let us say, and find the material interesting, the theme sympathetic, yet later feel our interest waning. The conclusion of the book seems to us flat and dull. Perhaps we cannot analyze what is wrong, but we are aware that somehow or other the story has been unsatisfactorily told. If we give the matter a little more thought— as novel-readers seldom do—we may be able to discover the source of the difficulty. In most cases it will prove to be a defect of presentation, for any kind of material can be made sufficiently interesting if treated in the right way. The novels of Arnold Bennett furnish as good an illustration of this as we have had in recent times. By his skill in managing detail and giving it relevance to his story he induced his great public to read with avidity what would have seemed most tedious stuff if handled by almost anyone else.

Or consider the many novels showing the development of a child to manhood or womanhood—

a kind very popular ever since Fielding's day. Not infrequently they begin extremely well but fail, as they proceed, to interest us. We feel a sense of anti-climax at what should be the most captivating stretch of the tale, when the hero or heroine has overcome the difficulties of adolescence and is emerging into the struggles of maturity. In such cases it usually will be found, I think, that the author has allowed himself to expand unduly the account of the hero's childhood and earlier youth, and has then scamped the chapters in which there should have appeared a mounting interest. Tension is relaxed, and the story slides downhill at a swifter and swifter pace to a flat conclusion. Examples of this sort of thing will occur to any experienced reader. No better proof could be found that form is not a negligible thing in fiction.

A second way to see that, in spite of the malleability of its material, fiction has to be shaped by the author is to note certain inevitable limitations of narrative. In another connection we have observed that a story can by no means reproduce life, or a slice of it, but can at best merely suggest it, represent it, illuminate it. In some respects fiction is less free to deal with life than is the play, which by its very nature requires dramatist and auditor to accept various conventions, or have no traffic with one another. Many things therefore cannot be done on the stage, and must be suggested —if at all—by roundabout means. Yet the play can represent actions as happening while the audience looks on and listens, which never can be done in a story. Fiction must always be retrospective. The tale has to be ended before it can be told. By no device can the view of life we get be anything but that of the past. The author can give us the contemporary scene, to be sure, but not quite that of to-day. The events that happen must have taken place at least yesterday, or last week, or—in the case of a printed book—at least last year. We may be satisfied that the cheek of the heroine still bears the flush of youth, but we cannot have revealed to us the secrets of her heart until she has ended the particular experience that captivates us, and has decided which man she will marry. The hero, young or middle-aged, may have gone through his trials and fought his battles very recently, but he has come to the end of them before we can be told what they are. Curiously enough, even if the scene of the story is laid in the future, the happenings have to be related as having already passed. We never can overtake the march of time in our fiction.

This limitation suggests other conventions, in which, as readers, we acquiesce because we must. Some of them, indeed, are shocking to common sense, just as it shocks common sense at the play to look into a room from which an entire wall has been removed by the producer. The modern novelist, for example, constantly assumes a knowledge of his characters' behavior at all points and throughout every hour of every day. The characters cannot escape his eye whatever they do or wherever they go. More than that, he penetrates their minds and reveals their secret thoughts and hidden motives. Obviously no human creature can have so complete a knowledge as this of any other creature, whether observed or bred from fancy. We accept the convention, in fiction as in drama, that the author possesses this knowledge, because it is useful to his art and furnishes us both pleasure and instruction. We say that he uses his imagination, and leave the matter at that; but by our acceptance we tacitly assume that fiction is truly an art like any other, with possibilities in the way of form as well as of substance.

Or we read a story ostensibly narrated by one of the characters. The real author's name is on the title-page of the book, and there is no attempt at hocus-pocus on his part or the publisher's. We understand perfectly well that the narrator is purely fictional, and that the whole transaction is on the plane of what I have called imagined reality. As we read, we assume that the supposed narrator will emerge from his adventures at the end of the tale, saddened by experience perhaps but unharmed. Yet our excitement is not diminished by this expectation. We put our trust in the author of the title-page, who takes over and by virtue of his occult powers gives to the world what the author in the story has revealed. Surely such a procedure as this implies some formalized management of material.

Fiction, in short, though it may not be controlled by fixed laws, must be shaped by the creator as much as the product of any other art, the only difference being that because of its complexity the formal possibilities are more extended. Satisfactory rules for the guidance of the author cannot be laid down, no matter how many text-books are written and courses of instruction mapped out; but the study of how stories have been made, the analysis of their elements, can do much to quicken in the reader a sense of values. It can help him, that is, to understand why one piece of fiction satisfies him as an interpretation of life and another does not, or it may perhaps stir him to dissatisfaction with stories of no consequence which he has been fooled into accepting at their face value.

Of the factors that contribute, or may contribute, distinction of form to fiction, the distribution of time and space may well be considered first, not because it is more important than some other things but because it reveals itself so clearly and simply. This was what Scott had in mind when he complained of his own work that in spite of repeated efforts to construct a novel "to scale . . . my regular mansion turns out a Gothic anomaly." Every novelist, whether or not he knows the end of his story when he begins to write it, has to imagine a sequence of events as he proceeds, and to relate them with greater or less completeness. Time moves forward with the action. The author's aim is to present an uninterrupted narrative, but he cannot by any possibility set down all the events, all the talk, all the thoughts that must have come to his characters between the imagined day when the story begins and the day it ends. He has to select, and he has to pass over in silence many periods of time: hours or days or months. Even though he confine himself to the happenings of a single day, as certain recent novelists have done by way of experiment, he still must make these omissions. His problem is one of giving the more significant points in the story due force by the use of circumstantial detail, whether of action or of dialogue, and yet of making his story something more than a series of loosely connected scenes. The proportion of space devoted to each particular turn of event, according, as it should, with its importance to plot or the elucidation of character, will determine his success in building what Scott called "a regular mansion."

The procedure inevitably will vary with the theme of the novel or romance, and with what the author is attempting to do with his material. Yet the story that is well made in this sense gives the reader a satisfaction which he does not get from equally great fiction less happily designed and less neatly executed. There can be no question as to the pleasure we derive from this source, even though we have not analyzed it and are completely unconscious of its nature.

Jane Austen's work is a case in point. Admirers have long praised what they call her "method." By this they mean nothing else than her unerring gift for devoting precisely the amount of space to a scene that its importance requires and for moving her readers forward smoothly from event to event at an even pace. If you will look attentively at *Pride and Prejudice*, for example, you will find that the elapsed time between scene and scene is seldom long. Miss Austen has imagined so very closely knit a sequence that we are conscious of no breaks. As a matter of fact, we notice the passage of time almost not at all; and we notice particular scenes only because one or another is especially witty or especially revealing, not because some are developed out of due proportion for the sake of dramatic emphasis or emotional appeal. So it is in all her books. The total effect of this nice construction is to give the reader a sense of completeness, a satisfied feeling that he has been shown all he needs to know about the Bennets, the Bertrams, or Emma Woodhouse. He has gained a full understanding of them. He has not been greatly excited perhaps, or deeply moved, but he has had an intellectual experience of the utmost value, and—let us hope—he has been in some measure affected by the beauty that inheres in a good design harmoniously wrought out.

Illustrations of quite another treatment of time and space may be found in novels that have no centralized themes, but instead use the biographies of heroes or heroines as their plots. *Jane Eyre* furnishes as good an example as one could desire of what may be done to give such material coherence and just proportion. The heroine tells her own story, a method of value, as we have seen, to the sense of reality that is attained. We follow Jane from the wretchedness of her childhood through many adventures to her marriage with Rochester. The narrative might well be very desultory and episodic. Under the guiding hand of Miss Bronte, however, Jane accommodates what she tells us about this or that period of her life to its importance in the completed design. Here she elaborates, there she sketches briefly or omits altogether, with the result that we read in a mounting fever of excitement. The emotional intensity of the story, together with the admixture of Gothic incident, is to some degree responsible for the suspense we feel, but without the precise and beautiful coordination of part to part it would lose much of its effect. No bolder stroke ever was made than that by which Miss Bronte passed over eight years of her heroine's life in half a dozen pages without breaking the continuity of the narrative. Jane had shown herself to us as a little girl so completely, had so established her personality in our minds, that the eight years before she left Lowood School needed no record beyond the briefest allusion. Not until she made her move to find a post as governess did the story require much telling. But only an author with a touch of genius could have resisted the temptation to let her recount the futilities of her adolescence. Somehow in the parsonage on the Yorkshire moors Charlotte Bronte learned what Jane Austen had learned in the parsonage at Steventon: how to write a novel that should have economy and beauty of design.

Fielding accomplished the same end as Miss Bronte in much the same way, although in *Tom Jones* he was working with a much larger canvas and was telling the story as author instead of letting one of his characters narrate it. Moreover, he plainly called attention to his procedure, knowing quite well what he was about. *Tom Jones* is divided into eighteen books. After the first two, which are introductory, Fielding indicated by captions the period of time covered by each. The third includes the events of three years, the fourth of one year, the fifth of somewhat more than six months, the sixth of three weeks, the seventh of three days, until at the height of the complications at the Upton inn only twelve hours pass during the course of Book X. This was no haphazard matter. It means that Fielding so planned the story that the events of weightiest moment received very full treatment, and therefore were developed within shorter periods of time, while things of minor importance were summarily dismissed. When one remembers that the characters of the novel are revealed in the action and by means of the action, the value of Fielding's nice craftsmanship becomes clear. Whatever is of exceptional importance to our knowledge of the young hero and his circle is shown in detail, whereas things that merely happened to them without much effect, or without much service to our understanding of them as individuals, are told briefly if at all. The story as a story, moreover, gains enormously in significance and interest through the symmetry of its construction. Countless novels have more ingenious plots than *Tom Jones*, but it would be hard to find anywhere a plot so well developed in action.

Great as is the value of such well-ordered construction as we have been discussing, it does not follow that a romance or a novel, in order to merit praise as work of art, must be composed after this fashion. The doctrine of *laissez-faire*, so dangerous in the field of economic practice, must be allowed to be quite satisfactory when applied to fiction. The most bigoted of pedants could not well deny to *Tristram Shandy*, in which confusion is supremely confounded, very delightful qualities as a novel; nor can one say, considering it maturely, that it lacks distinction of form. The truth is that form in fiction is not simply a matter of symmetry in construction but includes other very important elements. Indeed, the way a story ought to be told must vary with the material and the purpose of the tale. It would be absurd to demand that the author of a picaresque romance follow anything save the wandering picaresque formula. *Gil Blas*, or *Hajji Baba*, or *The Pickwick Papers* had to be what it is, invertebrate, in order to give the full savor of its astonishing episodes.

The interest of the reader in the outcome of a story—what we call suspense—is less dependent on careful organization than one would expect, and probably less than a conscientious author likes to think. Undoubtedly good construction increases our interest in the way a plot is going to turn, but it is not the main factor. Every confirmed reader of fiction must be aware of having been swept breathless through stories of adventure and through novels, which—soberly considered—were worthless. Empty of meaning, foolish of plot, feeble in character-drawing, barely literate in style, they yet have held us basely enthralled. The phenomenon deserves our thought. Interest of this kind, evidently, is not a safe index to the merit of a work of fiction, though every novel and every romance must have it to some degree. The successful author must captivate his readers' attention, and in most cases he does this by holding them in suspense as to the course the story is to take.

The suspense may be either one of two sorts, however. You may feel a continued and mounting interest in what is going to happen, or you may be sustained by the wish to find out how a foreseen conclusion is going to come to pass. Or, of course, you may be held by a combination of these motives. In reading a yarn of adventure you look chiefly for unexpected turns of fortune; in a detective story you are equally interested in the discovery of the murderer and the means by which his villainy is brought to light; but in many a good novel you know from the start what the fate of the hero and heroine is to be, yet find of absorbing interest the ways by which they come to it. Whenever the outcome of the story is determined chiefly by the qualities inherent in the characters, your attention is centered on their actions and reactions. Rightly, I think, the suspense created in this way is held to be a higher form than that induced by mystery and surprise. It requires more intelligence of the reader and is more stimulating to his imagination. Our feeling of suspense as to how Adam Bede or young Richard Feverel is going to face the difficulties he encounters is quite as acute as that induced in a tale of hairbreadth escapes, and it is based on something intrinsically more important than our love of excitement for excitement's sake.

Another thing we ought to keep in mind when considering how suspense may be created and sustained is this: it may be a play either for our minds or for our emotions. When we read an exciting detective story, for example, our feelings are not greatly stirred. Even if our flesh is made to creep by a writer who adds the spice of gruesome horror to the dish of mystery, we do not take the sensation very seriously. We know that *The Case of the Missing Slipper* is pure fantasy, that X the murderer is as artificial as the anise-seed bag hunted in a foxless country, and that the supremely ingenious detective has gifts beyond those of any mere man; yet we are absorbed by the tale because we like to follow through the complicated puzzle and are captivated by the unexpected turns of event. The appeal is wholly to our minds.

Oddly enough, a similar appeal furnishes the suspense in some of our best novels. As I have said before, Jane Austen does not excite us greatly, or at least does not excite us emotionally. She holds our absorbed attention by her revelation of a group of characters, who become better and better known to us as the story proceeds. The suspense she creates is chiefly intellectual. Or consider Henry James. We are genuinely and increasingly interested as we follow the story of Christopher Newman or Isabel Archer; what Maisie knew is so delicately revealed to us that our appreciation mounts as we learn more and more about the cobweb in which she is entangled. Yet we view the experiences of these people with a detachment like that of their creator. Our minds are stimulated, but our feelings are not deeply moved.

On the other hand, romances of adventure and novels of another stripe engage our emotions from the start and hold us in suspense by means of our emotions. There is mystery in *Treasure Island*, to be sure, but from the moment Bill Bones first appears at the Admiral Benbow and sings his terrifying chanty, Stevenson plays upon our feelings by device after device. The nature of emotional suspense cannot be studied to better advantage in any other book ever written. Dickens, again, with wholly different ends in view and wholly different material, enthralls us by similar means. He was clumsy in managing the complicated plots he often affected, and certainly he did not keep his audience in suspense by his mystery-mongering, taken by itself. But Dickens never let a plot stand on its own legs, any more than he let a character appear without the benefit of his peculiar and effective eccentricity of drawing. Plots and characters alike were highly emotionalized—so presented as to grip us at the start and keep us under the control of the author's fervid imagination to the end. Dickens was incapable of giving a plain, unbiased account of any man or any thing, but he was a great master in his power of intensification. By means of it he captures our attention, and carries us along on wave after wave of emotion through his splendidly dramatic narratives. Thomas Hardy deals in much the same way with us. He had, to be sure, the gift of constructing an extremely well-ordered story, which Dickens lacked; but he depended on emotional stresses to hold our interest, and through emotional stresses he made his novels mount from strength to strength to the crashing conclusions that stun us with their power, whether or no we can accept them as inevitable.

Quite another aspect of the problem of form in fiction is presented when we look at the units out of which stories are built up. Although the scene has not the same importance as in drama, since the story-teller has an opportunity denied the playwright of speaking in his own person as analyst, commentator, or reporter, it nevertheless is true that every tale—certainly every tale of considerable length—must have a backbone of events that are shown by means of conversation, with the characters moving about in a definite setting. In the choice of these scenes, as well as in the handling of them, much of the author's skill, or feebleness, is exhibited. No surer index to bad craftsmanship in a novel can be found than the elaboration of scenes that are merely illustrative and do little or nothing to advance the action. They may be ever so brisk in conversation, they may even show violent and exciting deeds, but if they do not tell us something new about the characters or help to move the plot towards a solution, they lack the essential quality. Without it, they are a burden to the story. A novel in which the scenes have no significance with reference to the development of characters and action may be read in its own time because the ideas it embodies are of contemporary interest or the emotions it describes are sympathetic to its immediate audience, but it is a dead thing and surely will be forgotten in a little while.

The quality of the author's imagination, together with his skill as a craftsman, is shown too in the way he treats the scenes he has chosen to use. The great masters, whether working in verse or in prose, always have had the power of seeing with the mind's eye more intensely and more completely

than other men. The gift is, indeed, the most essential element in what we call imagination. In
fiction it enables the writer to picture more vividly
the scenes he wishes to show than he can describe
events which he has observed in a physical sense.
Otherwise the great scenes of fiction would not live
in our memories as they do. Kipling, for example,
who was an extraordinarily good reporter of actualities, gave to the imagined scenes of *Kim* a
quality very much surpassing anything he wrote
about events he had witnessed.

No formula derived from past performances can
serve as a guide in this matter, nor is it easy to define except in the most general terms the characteristics of a scene that lift it out of mediocrity. We
recognize Thackeray's power in this respect, but we
do not find him following any set rules. Sometimes
he develops a scene with elaborate circumstance,
whether in comic or serious vein, letting us follow
the conversation and the movements of the characters—not without interpretative comments as
to what they are really thinking—through a cres-
cendo to some great climax of revelation; sometimes he is very casual with us, as if leading us into
a room where, privileged and innocent eavesdrop-
pers, we hear what is going on. On the whole he
reports rather fully, letting us get the effect he de-

sires to produce from what his people do and say. He does not often summon to his aid those adjuncts of the stage, of which Thomas Hardy made such magnificent use: the brooding melancholy of Egdon Heath, the heat of the day when Mrs. Yeobright died, the mystery of Stonehenge. We find another manner, again, in George Meredith, who seems less to be reporting complete scenes, even when there is much talk, than to be catching significant gestures and phrases out of the current of life that he has imagined for our pleasure. The writer of fiction, obviously, has a far greater latitude than the playwright in the treatment of his scenes, though he is equally dependent upon them in weaving the fabric of his story.

This fabric may be very simple or very complicated in design. The difference among novels with regard to this already has come to our attention in considering their structure. There is no inevitable virtue, I believe, in either complication or simplicity as far as longer pieces of fiction are concerned. The case is different with short stories, which must in the nature of things be less rather than more elaborate. Kipling, to be sure, could so distill the material of a novel that in a few thousand words he could give us most of the satisfactions and values to be found in a story filling a volume; but even Kipling had to make his sacrifices to brevity. Of necessity he implied far more than he told. Nearly all other masters of short tales in prose have simplified more than he, emphasizing at most no more than two of the three possible elements of fiction: plot, setting, and character. Some of the best of them, like Poe, have been content to depend on one of these elements only, in order to achieve what Poe himself called "a certain unique or single effect."

In longer works such simplification has been exceptional and never so extreme. Until about the middle of the nineteenth century any approach to it was dictated by the nature of the material used or by some idiosyncrasy of the author, and was not really a conscious effort. Defoe accomplished something of the sort by telling his stories in the first person and neglecting character—neglecting it, or using it in only a rudimentary way, no doubt, because he was incapable of looking beneath the surface of any other human creature than himself. Laurence Sterne simplified, too, in that everything he wrote was saturated with his own fantastic individualism, but in no other respect. Miss Austen, working neatly with small and circumscribed groups of characters, achieved a notable singleness of effect, but she had no theory except the good one that a novel ought to be a record of things as they are. With Scott appeared a rather shapeless and inclusive type of story, which not only was cultivated in Victorian England but has flourished ever since in France, Germany, Russia, and the United States as well. We may term it, for convenience, the conglomerate novel, since it is tolerant of all kinds of material and presents a motley surface. I have called such novels shapeless, and so they are. They may, however, and often do mirror the surfaces of life with extraordinary fidelity, and suggest the texture of life more effectively than any other kind.

About the middle of the last century a tendency appeared on the part of certain writers to mould serious fiction along simpler lines, to restrict the canvas, to limit the point of view. All these means were used to give sharper focus to the author's interpretation of his characters' motives and inner life. One sees the tendency in George Eliot, in Flaubert, in Meredith, in Henry James, in Conrad. It might have been expected that this simplification would lead to structural firmness, to careful organization—qualities not found in Dickens or Thackeray or Trollope. In Flaubert and George Eliot it had that effect, indeed, but not in their successors, even down to our own day. Instead,

the great attention they have given to what is mis-
called the "psychology" of their characters has
led such novelists more often than not into form-
lessness. The lack of form has been as striking in
their work, one finds, as in the conglomerate novel,
though it has manifested itself in different ways.
Despite the limitation of canvas at which he aimed,
Henry James plodded through his stories without
much grace; despite his singleness of aim, Joseph
Conrad seldom managed to avoid awkward twists
and turns. Since their time we have had both
Joyce and Proust, not to mention less extreme examples: novelists with unquestionable powers of
introspection and with very delicate intuitions besides, who have been quite unable to mould their
imaginings into any form whatever.

Were the tendency they represent a dominant
one, there would be little hope for the novel in the
immediate future, since they have pushed the convention of the author's omniscience to quite dis-
reputable lengths. There is always grave danger
that in attempting to reveal the inner life of a
group of imagined persons a writer will show only
different aspects of his own, giving introspection
too great play. Unless he objectifies the scenes and
the figures he is describing, viewing them with a
certain detachment and correlating personalities

with actions, he cannot well avoid this. Even though his conception of the characters has been sound at the start, he is liable to great confusion in treating them, with the result that all of them unduly resemble their creator. He spins an un-patterned web, which may seem at first sight very subtly made but leaves the reader bewildered. Soundness of character-drawing, one concludes, is closely linked with shapeliness of narrative struc-ture or at least with the power of projecting the thing imagined and keeping it always under con-trol. Mr. William Faulkner, I believe, notwith-standing the unusual delicacy of his perceptions and his gift of phrase, furnishes a contemporary instance of what I mean. Until he can learn to dis-criminate between reverie and imagination, he will continue to disappoint his admirers.

Throughout all fiction of real merit there appears an element which we have not yet considered ex-cept quite incidentally. No better name has been found for this than atmosphere, which is vague but serviceable. The quality it stands for results from the author's choice and treatment of plot, characters, and scene, all of which are colored in some degree by his personality. Samuel Richard-son, for example, surrounded all his work with a faintly sour and musty atmosphere, which is as characteristic as the clear light in which Jane Austen's people have their being. The setting does not wholly account for this. Fielding's country houses are in no essential different from Richardson's, but the wind blows fresh about them. At one time or another most novelists of the eighteenth century carried a group of persons to Bath, and faithfully described scenes at the famous watering-place, but not to the destruction of the atmosphere peculiar to himself. Each took his atmosphere with him.

With the rise of Gothic romance, however, a new significance was given to the use of atmosphere, chiefly because Sir Walter Scott adopted the fashion and ennobled it. Ever since his day both novelists and writers of romance have used the inanimate surroundings of their characters to give color and emphasis to their scenes. They have gained emotional heightening by picturing landscape and conditions of weather suitable to the mood they wished to induce in the reader; they have described buildings outside and inside with the same end— not simply ruined castles but houses great and small in good repair, and cathedrals, and village churches; in short, they have made the setting such an important constituent of every story that we have come to think of atmosphere as a matter of this background only. The limitation has had the unfortunate result of making authors, as well as readers, forget that the story itself and the people in the story should move us, irrespective of any trappings. Too many novels of the past hundred years have depended, for an effective interpretation of man, on natural scenery, on storm and sunshine, on things man has made. They are like buildings on which decoration has been lavished by the architects to cover up their poverty of design.

Yet in spite of such abuses it cannot be denied that atmosphere in the narrower modern sense has been and can be legitimately of great service in fiction. When a mood is proper to a character and a scene, it may well be emphasized by the conditions under which they are viewed. Scott was supremely right in making the use he did of Wolf's Crag in *The Bride of Lammermoor*, and of all the tempests and lonely dwelling-places that swarm in his novels. Hawthorne was right when he placed his characters in a House of Seven Gables. Dickens was right in letting the fogs of London darken the skies over Oliver Twist, and equally right in making the sun shine when Tom Pinch's sister walked abroad. Joseph Conrad could not have shown the passions of men and women with the power he did if he had not pictured the seas and the islands in consonance with them. Hardy, it is evident, needed the heaths and downs of Wessex against which to display the malignancy of the deity he worshipped.

Hardy, indeed, illustrates well both the usefulness and the danger of the appeal to nature in a story about human beings. The sombre beauty of his descriptions is beyond question, as is their effectiveness in imposing on the reader the mood desired; but the mood is sometimes imposed—in *Tess*, for example—on characters and in circumstances where it does not fit. Tess, endowed as she was by her creator with a placid temperament, could have endured her lot without too great unhappiness if only her creator did not make us feel by extraneous description that her lot was unendurable. In other words, Hardy—like many of his disciples—used decoration that was not functional. If further evidence be necessary, *Jude the Obscure* furnishes it. In this final effort he abandoned decoration altogether, leaving revealed his weakness as a maker of real tragedy. Which is not to deny that he wrote superb melodrama.

Last of all, but not because it is of least importance, we must note how much fiction owes to the style in which it is written. The modern novel, one is safe in asserting, could not have come into being until a suitable prose had been developed to serve as a medium. For this a long period of discipline in writing was required. The mannered styles of the sixteenth and seventeenth centuries were too ornate, and the plainer styles too little varied for the purpose. Chivalric romances and stories of adventure, real or feigned, were admirably embodied in these older ways of expression, but not until the eighteenth century approached was either English or any other European tongue ready for the use of the writer who would interpret the characters of men in prose fiction. If Rabelais and Cervantes are cited to prove the contrary, one can only reply that each of these men was a genius to whom all things were possible and that neither wrote a novel precisely of our modern sort.

Quite evidently, then, style is an important element in fiction, and must be taken into account in estimating the extent to which form matters in the art of making it. The same thing is true here that is true with regard to structure, character-drawing, and setting: the widest latitude is consistent with great performance, but neglect or shoddiness is not. Brilliant writing will not of itself make a novel good, but neither will any one of the other elements that constitute it—even the sound delineation of people to whom nothing significant happens. On the other hand, a lack of distinction in style will keep a novelist from reaching the peak of excellence where, on every other score, he belongs. It is regrettable, for example, that Anthony Trollope did not possess a greater mastery of prose. Not merely for the sake of the prose, however. The style, whatever it be, pervades the book; in a sense it *is* the book, because the story has no existence except through the words of which it is composed. The beauty and adequacy of the medium cannot fail to affect the tale in every part. It cannot make a bad novel good, as I have said, but it can heighten and deepen the impression that the author is attempting to convey. He cannot afford to neglect it if he aspires to be a master of his craft, nor should the reader fail to take it into account when estimating the value of a piece of fiction.

(4)

Ideas in Fiction

IN an earlier chapter I have said that certain readers always ask about a novel: "Is it informative?" or "Has it a good influence?" Such questions are perfectly legitimate, since serious writing cannot well be empty of ideas implied or expressed. The quest of "pure" literature, like similar quests in other fields of art, leads only to disillusionment. We need not scoff, then, at the questions, as readers who pride themselves on their sophistication always have been prone to do. They are questions which must be honestly faced if we are going to make any just appraisal of values in fiction. They are questions, however, much more easily asked than answered, for they present problems in criticism of a very complicated kind.

If we retort to the earnest reader: "Just tell me, please, what you mean by informative, or improving," we shall not clarify his thought or our own. It is altogether unlikely that he will be able to realize that he regards as improving only those ideas which accord with his fixed prejudices, and information agreeable only if it ministers to curiosities already awakened. Yet this, no doubt, is the truth. People who make the demand of fiction that it instruct and elevate usually lack much notion of its deeper purposes and lack correspondingly any sense of values in connection with it. We may surmise too that there underlie the demand reasons of which the readers in question are not conscious. They respond to the appeal of emotion quite as other readers do, but they are inhibited from unqualified enjoyment unless they can justify it on the score of intellectual or moral instruction.

You may say that I am picturing a kind of person who no longer lives—the puritan who is the butt of so much derision in our time. But the puritan has left descendants, who call themselves by different names and cling to different creeds, but are recognizable as belonging to the same family and exhibiting a well-defined set of inherited characteristics. They have a similar temper of mind: an inflexible belief in the rightness of their own ways of thinking, a rigid intolerance towards other opinions, and an earnest desire to make over the world according to a pattern of their own.

Sometimes they call themselves Communists, sometimes Liberty Leaguers, sometimes New Dealers, and sometimes—most oddly of all—Humanists. The great host of members of women's clubs and the majority of university professors belong to one or another branch of the family. These persons may read fiction for amusement and relaxation quite without thought of ideas, or the lack of them, but in novels that they take seriously they expect to find information of some kind and a point of view sympathetic to their own. Often they will read very dull contemporary books indeed, because they are told that truth is to be found in them—the political truth, the economic truth, the philosophical truth, the truth of destruction perhaps, or the truth of faith revived. Obviously all the tribe will not enjoy the same books, but they will enjoy in much the same way the things agreeable to their opinions. Sometimes, it is to be feared, they even read from no higher motive than imitative ostentation, counting boredom a small price to pay for the stamp of culture.

Yet ideas have an important place in fiction, and instruction of various kinds may well be conveyed by stories. So it has been since the great days of Hindu literature before our era began, and so it is to-day. Fiction, like the play, is an excellent medium for the exposition of problems that touch us all and for the dissemination of truth as men see it. In some ways fiction is an even better medium than the drama, since the author has a freedom to comment that is denied the playwright and may, if he pleases, develop his theme with more detail. Necessary conventions, as we have seen, are few. A writer can use material of the widest range and can treat it at his own will. He can write a bare apologue and make his point effectively, or he can develop it in an elaborate novel. With so much liberty possible, one might ask whether there can be any possibility of his going wrong—whether the worth of a piece of fiction does not lie in its having an idea at its core and on the value of that idea. May it not be that the puritans and their strangely assorted offspring are right in demanding instruction from stories, even though we cannot grant that they ought to minister to prejudice?

Obviously it is very easy to fall into confusion when thinking about ideas in fiction, for the matter is a complicated one. Unless we take care, we may find ourselves admitting absurdities or promulgating them. On the one hand, we must not deny the part that ideas rightly play, but on the other we must not forget that a wholly worthless book may be written on a theme of the highest importance. The intellectual content of a novel certainly is no safe index to its value as fiction. *The Ordeal of Richard Feverel* cannot be rated a greater work than *Wuthering Heights* simply because it expresses the well-considered opinions of the brilliant author on a topic which every generation must ponder anew. The relative merits of the two books, if they were to be compared at all, would have to be decided on quite other grounds. Everyone will concede, nevertheless, that *Richard Feverel* is somehow a more important novel, in and of itself, because of the central idea by which it is dominated. *Wuthering Heights* has no such intellectual core, and needs none, being a heightened and yet poignantly truthful representation of love and hatred unbridled.

What place, then, do ideas have in fiction, if they are essential in one masterpiece, while another is empty of them? This is the question we must try to answer.

In working out a solution of the problem it will be best, I think, to determine in the first place whether the same conditions hold for all kinds of stories, and whether the modern novel does not stand on a different footing in this matter from other fiction. Perhaps the distinction I have in mind can best be understood by contrasting two

simple but magnificently executed narratives of
Holy Writ. The tale of Jezebel in the *Books of the
Kings* recounts in outline the history and death of
that barbaric queen. The episodes of her life are so
well selected that we get from them a sense of knowing not only the whole story but the character of
a woman who had the courage of her masterful
wickedness. It is the distillation of an entire novel.
Yet, though moral issues aplenty are involved in it,
and though it has furnished thousands of preachers
with themes for discourses, it cannot be said to
focus on any generalized idea. It is the tale of a
very interestingly bad woman, that is all: the tale
of an individual—a concrete case.

On the other hand, consider the parable of the
Good Samaritan in the *Gospel of Luke*. The story
is complete, satisfying, unforgettable—one of the
best in the world. Yet the Good Samaritan, though
he stands for all time as the figure of human mercy,
is not an individualized creature like Jezebel. In
other words, he and the man who went down from
Jerusalem to Jericho and the Levite who passed by
on the other side were invented, together with the
things that happened, to illustrate a certain point.
The story is a parable. It exists to teach a specific
lesson and owes its effectiveness to the subordina-
tion of everything else to that one purpose. It could

not be improved, certainly, by giving names and personalities to the three stark figures. The idea it embodies is explicit. It is thus altogether different from the story of Jezebel, which implies many things but is not told to impress upon us a single idea.

Let us put the matter tentatively in these general terms: a story the chief interest of which lies in incident can be used to illustrate an abstract notion without any difficulty whatever, whereas a story depending for its interest chiefly on the thoughts and behavior of individualized human beings cannot without considerable danger be so used. The parable, the fable, the utopian romance, and the like may be excellent narratives, and yet not represent particularized men and women at all. The story therefore does not have to grow out of the qualities, good or bad, attributed to the characters, does not depend upon the choices they make. They must conform to something resembling human speech and behavior, or they seem absurd, but they need have no marked individuality. The story may be invented solely to prove the point the author has in mind.

Dr. Johnson's *Rasselas* illustrates perfectly how such a tale may be dominated by an idea. *Rasselas* is a mere apologue to show the vanity of the pursuit of happiness, and pretends to be nothing else. The young Prince of Abyssinia is put through a series of adventures and conversations well calculated to disillusion him. His observations, as well as the things of which he is told, all have that one object. The story is simply a convenient vehicle. Much the same thing is true of Voltaire's *Zadig* and *Candide*, except that they serve the purpose of satire as well as philosophizing. They are livelier than *Rasselas* because informed by the author's malicious wit, but they are far from being stories told for the stories' sake. This does not in any way detract, however, from their importance as pieces of literature.

Gulliver's Travels provides an illuminating case of a similar but slightly different sort. The book is quite as much a vehicle of ideas as *Rasselas*, but it is also—at least in the first two voyages—a romance of fantastic adventure told with such sobriety of detail that the reader accepts the incredible because it scarcely can be distinguished from the matter of fact. The book is the bitterest of satires on man and all his ways and works, yet so captivating a romance that no child ever yet has paid much attention to the cynicism that permeates it. Swift has been no corrupter of youth; he has not sullied the pure waters of any childish imagination or dissipated any trailing clouds of glory. No better instance could be found to illustrate with what freedom the romancer may treat ideas and build his story about them. It is noteworthy that not even Lemuel Gulliver is sharply individualized. He is rather an epitome of traits that Swift recognized as belonging to adventurous and sensible Englishmen of his time. We are not so much interested by Gulliver as by the extraordinary observations he made in the course of his travels.

The Pilgrim's Progress is another work, the success of which depends to a considerable extent upon what may be called the thinness of the figures and their lack of individuality. Christian, his companions, and the people he meets by the way are admirably drawn in a visual sense and embody altogether human traits, but they are stiff after the fashion proper to allegory. If they were represented like the characters of a modern novel, the story would become absurd, instead of being one of the noblest pieces of fiction in all literature. John Bunyan had a definite purpose in view, and— man of genius that he was—he hit upon the means by which he could enforce his religious lesson without the least sacrifice of truth as he saw it. His book can be read equally well as a tract and as a romance, for it is both; but it would not have the virtue it possesses as a tract if it were not a great work of fiction.

That ideas can have a place in tales of adventure, when there is no question either of satire or of propaganda, may be seen in the work of Defoe. In most ways *Robinson Crusoe* is no better a story than *Captain Singleton* or *Moll Flanders*. The adventures are no more surprising, nor is the detail more credible. Yet it has been a greater favorite throughout the generations, and deservedly so. Its superiority is in its theme: one of the best ever hit upon by a writer of fiction. No boy or man can resist the appeal of this. Set an ordinary human being to cope unaided with the forces of nature, and see how he fares. The more ordinary and colorless he is, the more effective will be the tale. Crusoe may be a mere projection of Daniel Defoe, who himself is a person very hard to understand, but he is a projection of those elements only which Defoe shared with millions. And he is unobtrusive. He does not get in our way when we wish to sequester ourselves on the lonely island and experience the adventures in our own right. Yes, *Robinson Crusoe* is a better book because of the idea on which it is founded.

Ideas in Fiction

You will notice that most of the illustrations I have been using are taken from fiction written before the novel had become a common form. Romance of one sort or another, open or disguised, was still what men read. Since the days when LeSage and Smollett, between them, taught the world how to combine the pleasures of getting an intimate acquaintance with imagined people and of following through a story of adventure, romancers seldom have been content to make their characters mere colorless figures but have tried at least to represent them as individuals. They have tried, that is, to be novelists as well as spinners of yarns. When they have used their stories as vehicles of specific ideas, they have accordingly encountered the dangers that novelists face in the same circumstances. We have seen that these dangers are not present if the story does not depend for its interest chiefly on the thoughts and behavior of individualized men and women. The author can then build his tale on the foundation of ideas without loss of the kind of verisimilitude he needs to achieve. Such is not the case, however, if his aim is that of human portraiture. The dangers become quite specific. Let us see what they are, and why they exist.

There is the danger, first of all, that he may mistake general information for information relevant to the story in hand, and interlard his narrative with extraneous material. This bad habit—of describing or discussing things that have nothing whatever to do with the main course of the book or with the understanding of the characters—has been observable ever since the eighteenth century, but much more frequently since the writers of Gothic romance discovered and transmitted the art of using settings to increase the emotional stress of their scenes. The connection between the two may not be immediately obvious, but its reality will be seen by noticing that historical novels and novels of propaganda have been the two kinds of fiction most grievously affected by the plague of information. In both cases description of things quite without value to the story itself has too often been inserted with the earnest but vain hope—one must suppose—of killing two birds with one stone. The author has thought to educate or convince his readers, and at the same time to captivate them, by other means than those proper to his craft.

Observe what has happened with historical fiction. Sir Walter Scott, who was a great artist, took over from Gothic romance many of its devices, including elaborate settings and the detailed descrip-

tion of events, which furnished the environment
for his characters. Thus he wove his magnificent
tapestries, making the past live again in them, and
stirring his readers by pageantry, as well as by the
truth to human nature which his men and women
reveal in what they say and do. But in spite of the
ingenuous lavishness with which Sir Walter used
these means, he was not primarily educative or
informative in his intent. He was trying to show,
and did show, the stuff of life by telling stories that
would give pleasure to his readers. What remains
in our memories when we have finished *The Heart
of Midlothian* is not the Porteous riots so much as
Jeanie Deans; what we recall from *The Fortunes
of Nigel* is less the wonderful re-creation of Alsatia
than the fumbling youth of the hero, together with
such figures as George Heriot and King James. In
the Waverley novels the settings never usurp the
place of the story; the atmosphere really is atmosphere; even in writing *Ivanhoe* and *The Talisman*
Sir Walter did not confuse the rôles of historian
and story-teller.

Of all too many of his followers, however, the
same cannot be said. Dumas can be acquitted of
the indictment, and so, despite his flaccid style,
can James Fenimore Cooper; but Victor Hugo—
notwithstanding his great gifts—stands accused.

As for Harrison Ainsworth and Bulwer and Charles Kingsley and Charles Reade and Tolstoi and Mr. Hervey Allen, to name only a few of the delinquents, there is a lack of proper integration between setting and story. The informative background tends to become foreground, while the persons of the tale remain mere puppets, the strings of which are too obviously pulled by the author. This feebleness in characterization would not so much matter of itself, since there is every reason to respect and enjoy a story frankly conceived as an historical romance. The early books of Maurice Hewlett were charming things in this kind, as in another way were the prose tales of William Morris. Unfortunately, however, the novelists we are considering have not been content to do this sort of thing. They have wished to present rounded characters, and they have permitted a device intended to vivify human action to become so over-burdened with informative detail as to destroy its own effectiveness. This has driven them, on the one hand, to a weak and false emotionalism and, on the other, to melodramatic exaggeration in the handling of both characters and situations. Not infrequently the two tendencies have been present in the same book.

Ideas in Fiction

The results have been altogether deplorable, the more so that such novels have been very popular. They have vitiated taste, for one thing, by seeming to be what they are not: sound representations of life at one or another period of the world. Readers have been deceived into believing themselves attracted by the knowledge placed within their grasp, though they really have responded to the appeal of sentimentalism and crude melodrama. Undoubtedly the archaeological and historical accuracy of some of Scott's successors has been much greater than Sir Walter's, but this has not compensated for their essential defects. They have gone wrong, and critics have gone wrong in estimating their work, through failing to understand what information can contribute to fiction and what it cannot. In a word, they have not realized that a novel can be a proper vehicle of ideas only if the ideas are imaginatively fused in the stuff of the story itself. In the historical novel, certainly, the setting must support the action and help to interpret the characters; characters and action must not be devised to fit the setting.

In an earlier chapter I have paid my respects to one story of the kind, which was undeservedly famous in the nineteenth century—*The Cloister and the Hearth*. A couple of other examples will serve to make my argument clear. Look for a moment at Bulwer's *Rienzi*. Bulwer was a most competent man of letters, as well as an industrious one. He never wrote a novel that was worse than second-rate, and occasionally, he achieved something of permanent worth, though not in this kind. *Rienzi* is typical of his historical fiction, which has had wide and long-continued popularity. The career of his hero, the Roman tribune, furnished him with an admirable subject. Unfortunately he was unable to keep the setting in the right perspective and relied on heightened emotional stresses and violent action to counteract the effect of the pompous historical essays with which the book is interlarded. It is a sign of the essential feebleness of the treatment that, in spite of the gusto which never failed Bulwer, he sometimes evaded scenes that should have been the high spots of his story. Charles Kingsley's *Westward Ho!* is an even more deplorable case, though it is a book still given boys and girls to read in many schools, presumably because of the information about Elizabethan England to be derived from it. Kingsley had no gift for drawing characters that were consistently imagined, no gift for story-telling, but he covered up his poverty by such a flaming cloud of overwrought emotionalism that he still deceives the adolescent in age or mind. The lushness of the elaborate descriptive passages in *Westward Ho!* does not redeem them. If you will examine them with a little care, you will see at once that they are used to enforce the protestant antipathies and the violent feelings of the clerical author, and that they never are truly integrated with the story.

As I have said, novels of propaganda—of purpose, to use a commoner but less accurate term— have been similarly afflicted by the curse of information. The trouble has been accentuated in them by the desire of the authors not only to explain conditions but to persuade their readers that such conditions are intolerable and must be altered. Settings have been as important and intrusive as in the historical novels at which we have been glancing, but frequently even worse in what they have done to the imaginations of the writers, since they have been elaborated not for the sake of showing the characters to better advantage but simply to display the evils that surround them. A novel of propaganda must in the nature of things have a bias, and it must be so constructed as to show certain things to be very wrong and other things to be supremely right. The author cannot be the detached observer. We must expect him to be extremely earnest. Yet on account of his earnestness, more often than not, he fails to represent men and women as they are. What should be the setting becomes the story, and the characters become the setting. They tend to be mere automata, constructed—not created—to fit the thesis the author is expounding.

A reasonably just empirical test of the snares that beset the novelist with a purpose is found in the rapidity with which most of their books become out of date. Even though exceedingly popular when they first appear, they fade sooner than other novels to the making of which equal intelligence has gone. Generally speaking, their authors have something to say, and have thought as well as felt. They may even be the admired prophets of their generation. Yet to the generations that follow they are lingering memories at best, and subjects for curious scholarship. This is due in some measure, no doubt, to the fact that the information they purvey has no longer anything but historical interest, and that the burning questions of one day blacken like cinders the next, when the fire has gone out of them. More important than this, however, is the danger, just mentioned, of the author's being more interested in his ideas than in his story and the people of his story. Too often it happens that his characters never come to life; and when the immediate interest of the theme has passed, the book is dead.

Call the roll of influential novels of propaganda from Godwin's *Caleb Williams* to Mrs. Ward's *Robert Elsmere* and Gissing's *New Grub Street* at the end of the nineteenth century. Very few of them are read nowadays except by students interested in the history of fiction or in social history, nor do they merit reading. The brilliant mind of Disraeli has not preserved *Coningsby* or *Sybil*. The careful documentation of Charles Reade did not make *Hard Cash* and *Put Yourself in His Place* sound novels. As for the earnestness of Charles Kingsley and the fanatic enthusiasm of Mrs. Harriet Beecher Stowe, the most one can say is that they made those writers effective propagandists in their time. It is the same to-day. Mr. H. G. Wells, in spite of unwearied energy and unusual gifts, has been able only two or three times to escape the domination of a thesis and give his creative imagination free play. *Kipps* and *Tono-Bungay* have a chance of survival—of giving pleasure and food for thought to a later generation—beyond that of the long series of books by which they have been succeeded. For similar reasons Mr. Sinclair Lewis usually has failed to produce novels worthy of his powers. He has been satirist and exhorter, and all too often has patterned his characters by his thought rather than by his imagination. In *Babbitt*, however, the creative fusion took place. The hero may possibly have more of Mr. Lewis in his make-up than does the typical American business man, but he is the representation of a living creature—not a man of straw.

We hear a good deal in these days about something called the proletarian novel, as if the use of fiction as an instrument of propaganda were a new phenomenon and likely to give health to the *genre* as well as to the body politic. No right-minded person can question the value to letters and to the state of having both young and old take thought about the problems of the world. No one ought to deny to authors the right to feel strongly about the opinions they hold. Personal bias and partisan fervor cannot be deplored. Good novels need something more than this, however. Writers with a social or political purpose, whether bourgeois or proletarian, must beware of manufacturing stories and characters to fit their preconceived ideas instead of contriving to embody their ideas in human terms. They must not write tracts and call themselves artists.

They should reflect upon the work of Charles

Dickens, though it may not be desirable that they imitate him except in one particular. Dickens could not help trying to right the wrongs of the world. From the beginning to the end of his career he was a propagandist. Even in *The Pickwick Papers* he showed himself a satirist and reformer. Nor was he always a just critic: he exaggerated and distorted; he thundered at abuses after the need of thundering was past. Yet his novels have not suffered the fate that has overtaken so many others. Their interest is perennial. They have not aged with the passage of time, but have an undiminished appeal to-day when the last of them have been in print for more than two generations. When one examines them to see how they differ from the long line of dead and dying novels of purpose, the reason for their survival is clear. Dickens was a propagandist, but he was a propagandist chiefly because he saw the havoc wrought by various abuses on men, women, and children. He saw the world in terms of flesh and spirit, not of ideas. He saw the evils of child labor not as an economic problem, but as something that ruined the lives of individual boys and girls who were quite real to him. He saw the delays and inadequacies of the courts as a menace to the security of people who thought and felt like himself and his readers. When he viewed

the ill-run private schools of his day, he envisaged
Dotheboys Hall and Mr. Squeers. In a word, he
was primarily a novelist, and a propagandist because he was a novelist—not a novelist because he
had ideas to expound. He did not write tracts, but
fiction.

From our consideration of historical novels and
novels of propaganda it has become clear, I hope,
that the use of fiction as a vehicle of ideas is at-
tended by some dangers but that these are not
fatal. On the contrary, a central problem which can
be stated abstractly, though not essential, may
well add to the significance of a story. Is it not on
this account that we reckon *Vanity Fair* the best
thing done by Thackeray? Does not Jane Austen's
mounting fame, as the generations go by, rest in
part on her simple themes, sometimes expressed in
her titles? *Pride and Prejudice* is not marred by the
presence of the idea so neatly developed. George
Meredith always focused his novels in this way,
which must be accounted a virtue in them, since
otherwise they would have far too little coherence.
There is a problem in each. What happens when
generous youth is held on too tight a rein? What
happens when a free spirit gets tangled in the net
of an outworn code? What, after all, makes a man
a gentleman? Or we are shown how one vice cor-

rodes the whole of a man. Henry James, too, in his more successful books had explicit themes, and Conrad often did. And is not the great superiority of Butler's *The Way of All Flesh* to most of the novels about families that have followed it due in great measure to the centralizing motive?

There are problems in all these novels, which is to say that each has an idea at its core and is not merely a slice of life. In a sense, all good stories that illuminate human relations by developing a given situation have such ideas imbedded in them, but one cannot say that it is always explicit, as it is in the cases I have just mentioned. The important thing to notice about these is that the theme is not imposed on the story, but that the idea is made manifest in the story itself. The story, the concrete group of characters, and their behavior are what matter to us while we read. Only as we reflect on the total representation do we see the book as illustrating an abstract principle.

Ideas treated in this way never have made a novel the worse, though it cannot be said that they are necessary to distinguished and enduring work. Only by casuistry could one argue for the existence of such a centralized idea in Fielding's *Tom Jones*. The book is a study of adolescence, to be sure, and the hero an epitome of male youth in the contradictions of flesh and spirit that he shows. In essentials he is youth itself, aspiring to goodness and yet the prey of ignoble desires, generous and yet selfish, strong of heart and yet pitiably weak. In a larger sense he is man undisciplined by experience. Fielding has drawn him for all time. There is thus no reproach whatever in saying that the novel has no abstract problem at its heart. The concrete case of Tom is so masterfully presented that it becomes universally significant, which is all we have any right to ask.

George Eliot illustrates the same point. Surely she took her vocation as novelist most seriously. For years, you will remember, she agonized over *Middlemarch*. No light scribbler she, but a woman of great intelligence and very considerable learning, who was so earnest about her art that she came dangerously close to regarding herself as inspired. She worked, too, along the lines of the science that was new in her day. Yet her themes in *Adam Bede* and *Middlemarch* are not ones that can be stated abstractly. She was bent on representing and interpreting human beings in the light of her experience and intuitive knowledge, but as themselves, not as embodying any idea. Many problems of behavior—many ethical problems withal—are worked out in her novels, yet always because they arise from the situations in which she has imagined her characters. No single idea dominates any one of her books.

Her procedure, however, does not differ in any essential way from that of the novelists who with real success have focused their stories on themes that can be stated in abstract terms. There, I believe, we come to the heart of the matter. A novel, to have lasting value, must be a tale of particularized men and women, not of man and woman in general. If it presents a problem, the problem must be incorporated in the stuff of the story, not imposed on the story. The story, that is, must not be moulded to fit the idea, but must seem at least to work itself out as do human lives, sometimes to predictable ends, sometimes in ways that baffle understanding. Ideas, of whatever sort, must be subordinate to this one end. If they come to be more important to an author than the people he is imagining, something is sure to go wrong with his work. He may be a useful teacher or preacher or prophet perhaps, and he may lay up for himself thereby treasure both in earth and heaven, but he will never join those immortals who have made of the novel so noble a medium for the interpretation of mankind to man.

This may seem to be taking high ground. If novels can be of use by way of spreading information about the present and the past, or by way of promoting discussion of the problems that torment every generation, why should we care about their quality? What does it matter, provided they interest readers at the moment of publication, that they are dead in five years or fifteen? Everyone knows that most books fail to survive infancy, though the corpses of many are preserved in libraries. Every writer acknowledges, unless his head has been turned by flattery, that the children of his brain have small chance of living very long. The novelist, like the playwright, must in any case try to give enjoyment, and perhaps profit, to his own generation and leave the rest to time. Is it of consequence if Mr. Sinclair Lewis, in order to impress upon his readers the horrors of fascism, puts his hero through a sentimentalized love affair that smells of the gas lights under which it was first imagined long ago? The story is thus provided with the sex appeal without which, according to the formula triumphantly established by Mr. Wells and the late Mr. Galsworthy, no novel of ideas can be successful. Has not Mr. Charles Morgan recently proved by two works that even metaphysics of a sort, when administered with strong doses of sex and sentimentality, can be sold in quantity? In a word, need we ask anything more of a novelist who has pretensions to seriousness than that he furnish information and ideas compounded with whatever stereotyped fictional devices will catch the popular ear at the moment?

We must grant that such stories will continue to be written and published—produced in all good faith, no doubt—and that they will be hailed as masterpieces by the critics who are wholly immersed in the currents of the hour. Since the novel is such a convenient medium, this state of things is unavoidable. Accordingly the reader who cares for fiction as a product of man's artistry and an instrument for the interpretation of humanity to itself, who cares for wisdom even more than knowledge, will watch himself and his responses while reading the work of his contemporaries. He will take care, too, lest the *zeitgeist*—a dangerous creature not altogether Germanic of blood, or even Aryan— stupefy him with the fumes of propaganda that it breathes forth. Only by so doing will he be able to distinguish between a truthful representation of men and women and one that is essentially false, particularly when a novel is designed to provide information or set forth ideas. Even by taking pains the reader scarcely can hope to escape being fooled some of the time, but he will not so often be the dupe of contemporary and evanescent fashions.

To apply to the novel a utilitarian standard merely, to say that its functions are to amuse us or to furnish us information and nothing more, is to deny values proved through two centuries. These functions it has. It can give us opportunity to escape from ourselves and wander abroad through time and space quite as well as does the romance, but always through a world inhabited by men and women. It can make us see how people have lived and how they live now, what problems they meet and what discouragements they encounter in trying to solve them. It can present never-changing conflicts of the human heart in an ever-changing world. It is receptive of new ideas, and must be so, since each generation demands its own interpretation of life by its own interpreters. But none of these ends can be accomplished unless the makers of fiction keep steadily before them the true goal of their efforts as novelists, which must be always a picture of men and women as they are. This is the one thing needful. Ideas there must be, and the more and the newer the better; but they must emanate from the story itself, and they must not be permitted to obscure the main end. The novel of the future, like the novel of the past, must report the destinies of individuals, and by reporting them honestly serve as a criticism of life.

(5)

The Reader and the Author

IN what has gone before I have not, I hope, made the assumption or anywhere implied that fiction is a product of spontaneous growth. Whatever the story may be, whatever its form, whatever the ideas it expresses, some man or woman has imagined and shaped it. We shall do well to examine this simple truth in some detail, for it has implications of considerable importance.

In retrospect we may be able to see that certain fashions of writing have been influenced by events of historic interest. We may say, for example, that the Industrial Revolution affected the novel in the nineteenth century, and in a sense we are right in saying this. Only we ought to remember that the influence on the novel was secondary: the primary effect was on the novelists. Writers of fiction cannot free themselves from the currents of life that are flowing while they are at work, and it would be a pity if they could. They respond, sometimes consciously but more often without knowing it, to contemporary patterns. Yet each is a creator in his own right, each creates in his own way. No matter how mechanical the product may seem to an unsympathetic reader, there has gone into it the labor of some individual's imagination. The story-teller is, indeed, as truly a maker as the poet.

It is right for us, then, to analyze—we who are readers—the function of the novelist or romancer. We shall better understand and appreciate what he writes if we can see his relations to his material and to ourselves; and we ought in common justice to recognize our obligations to him. For a story is not simply a matter of so many thousands of words printed in a book: it is a cooperative affair. The writer of fiction has to persuade us to a game of make-believe with him. By various devices he has to cajole us into reconstructing the characters and scenes which he has imagined. Our imaginations must be set working in unison with his. By no possibility can he show us his people in the flesh, as the dramatist with the help of actors pretends to do. Unless he stimulates us to view with the inner eye what he has seen with his own fancy, there will be no representation at all. In a very real sense, the novel or romance does not exist except as the reader does his part and completes the transaction. The printed book is merely a mechanical device whereby what was in the author's mind is conveyed to ours.

It follows that we must acquiesce in his moods and submit ourselves to his guidance. Unless we do so, we cannot possibly receive the story that he has tried to transmit to us. We can follow the stages of the plot, to be sure, and perhaps get some notions about the characters; but we can by no means participate in the imaginative experience that the author has gone through. In other words, if we cannot or do not reconstruct a story in our own minds on the basis of the hints of the author, we are not reading it at all: we are merely reading about it.

Since the story is the writer's own invention, we must, moreover, accept it on his own terms—see it with his eyes. If he views his characters with detachment, as Jane Austen does, we must assume the same attitude towards them. If, like Balzac, he considers them as figures in the social fabric, we must do the same. If he presents them after the fashion of Dickens with all their features distorted, we must accept them as they appear. If in the manner of Thackeray he chooses to stroll about among the creatures of his imagining, looking at them now in one light and now in another, sometimes regarding them with satiric irony and sometimes with tender sentiment, we must follow in his steps and look at them with similar variability. The failure to observe this simple rule has led to more misunderstanding and more futile criticism, I believe, than any other of the numerous inadequacies through which writers of fiction have suffered at the hands of their readers.

The cooperation of reader with author does not imply that our critical sense need go to sleep. Somewhat as the writer in the act of composition must control his imagination, if he is to accomplish anything of value, rejecting this as wrong and choosing that as right, we can with due humility recognize that the guide to life whom we are following has here made a misstep or there quite badly stumbled. Only the naïf play-goer fails to preserve a certain detachment as he watches a spectacle on the stage. The wiser auditor may be absorbed in the drama, and certainly he must let his imagination respond to that of playwright and actors; but he is at the same time able to evaluate the effect produced—even the effect on his own feelings. He does not try to shoot the villain. Just so the experienced reader keeps his critical judgment awake while he yields himself to the guidance of the author. Nor is his enjoyment lessened by so doing. Indeed, he comes into closer association with the writer, and participates more fully in the imaginative processes by which the story has been made, if he combines such control with sympathetic absorption.

I have stressed the relationship of reader to author because a clear notion of it is necessary in considering the function of the writer of fiction with reference to his audience and to his material. He has no reason for being, in fact, except to minister to an audience. The lyric poet may have some excuse, perhaps, for thinking that he composes for himself alone, creating harmonies of sound and thought irrespective of any other person; but the story-teller, whether he writes in prose or verse, cannot by any possibility cherish such a belief. He creates whatever he creates in order that others may share his imaginative experience. The nature of his art requires him to keep an audience in mind, and therefore conditions not only the material he presents but the way in which he presents it. Communication is essential.

Since the reader, as we have seen, has to co-operate with him before the transaction is completed, it follows that a peculiarly intimate bond is established—at least in theory—between author and audience. This is especially true of prose fiction. The writer of an epic may be supposed to declaim his story publicly, but the prose romancer or the novelist is recounting his in private. He is thus free to adopt a conversational manner, as if the reader were by his side and were listening. A good deal of the charm that fiction has for modern readers comes from the intimacy established by this means. The novelist, if he knows his business, never condescends to us and never excludes us from the narrower circle of his friends. He invites us to sit down in the same room with him and reveals all the secrets about our fellows that he has been able to discover. He tells us of their tragic mistakes, of their absurd adventures, of their desires thwarted by fate or brought to a happy fulfilment; and he tells us these things with extraordinary candor. Only to the closest friend would he talk with such freedom.

Recall, for example, the intimacy of Laurence Sterne with his readers. What with his winks and his nudges, and his habit of dropping his voice altogether and leaving the rest to silence, *Tristram*

Shandy ought to be read only in the privacy of one's own room. But even better illustrations of what I mean can be found in authors whose inhibitions were stronger than those of Sterne. Look at George Eliot. A certain austerity of temper, a fixed resolve to account for all the mental and moral qualities of her characters so that none of their actions need be debatable, her grave earnestness in short, did not prevent her from telling things in her fiction that she could not have uttered during a general conversation in her drawing-room. With pen in hand she could unbosom herself much more freely than in other circumstances. Or think of the shy Bronte sisters, who were anything but shy when they wrote their stories. It is quite clear, too, that Nathaniel Hawthorne never could have said in a Concord parlor or study what he put into *The Scarlet Letter*.

Various devices have been adopted by writers of fiction to further the sense of intimacy of which I have been speaking. Henry Fielding set the fashion of addressing the reader in confidential terms, and he has been followed in the practice by a host of other novelists, both small and great. Who can forget the sentence that opens the concluding chapter of *Jane Eyre?* "Reader, I married him." It is perhaps the best example one could find to illustrate a relationship triumphantly established. Although the address to the reader has not been much employed of late, probably because authors have felt that it interferes with an objective treatment of scenes and characters, I have no doubt that it will come into fashion again, for it is a useful device.

Another means to the same end is the use of the first person in telling a story. No doubt writers have chosen this method primarily for the sake of the specious air of reality it gives a tale, but often they have adopted with it a tone of familiarity, letting the supposed narrator talk or write as if to a friend. One wonders whether the epistolary form of the novel, so popular in the eighteenth century, did not go out of fashion partly because it does not permit the close association of authors with readers that both classes apparently have craved. By recording in letters what has happened a sense of reality is established, but at the expense of any direct contact with the reader. The story tends to become a case history, with a consequent submergence of the author's personality.

In general, it must be said, the writer of fiction almost inevitably reveals himself as fully as any of his characters, which is one very important reason why his art is popular. He cannot well disguise himself even though he makes some fictitious personage tell the story. His own qualities appear in twenty ways—in material, in structure, in style. He cannot establish contact with his readers without doing so, for his is an intimate art, an art of privacy. No creator can fail, of course, to show himself through what he creates, but the maker of fiction does so more fully than most others. Quite apart from autobiographical reminiscences which he may incorporate in a tale, everything he writes is colored to an unusual degree by what he is. His intuitions and his instincts control both his imaginings and the manner in which he displays them. As readers we enjoy this self-revelation. Whether we realize it or not, we like the intimate contact established between ourselves and the author.

Or else we dislike it extremely, as sometimes is the case. Much of the adverse criticism from which great novelists have suffered has been the result of a temperamental antipathy between the particular critic and the particular author. The long-continued quarrel, for instance, between the admirers of Dickens and Thackeray—absurd enough in view of the transcendent merits of both writers

—has been due to nothing else. Some people do not like Dickens, and some people find Thackeray unsympathetic to them; and each party has been blind to the values esteemed by the other. Such acrimonious partisanship would not have been possible if Dickens and Thackeray did not reveal themselves so clearly in every chapter they wrote. Sex enters into it, too. Women, I have noticed, seldom feel a whole-hearted enthusiasm for Henry Fielding; but they are the most ardent admirers of Charlotte Bronte.

The odd fluctuations in popularity which great novelists go through, corresponding to shifts in commonly accepted points of view, indicate in another way how much we are affected by personalities. There was a time when George Eliot repelled intelligent readers, though now she appears to be coming into favor again. Meredith is at present suffering a period of eclipse because so many persons in England and America are put off by characteristics of his that seemed attractive a generation ago. Only by cultivating catholicity of temper and wide tolerance can one find real enjoyment in the undisputed classics of fiction, for without those qualities the reader will find himself frequently disliking books that his reason tells him he ought to admire.

One cause, undoubtedly, for the feeling of intimacy produced by the masters of story-telling is the malleability of narrative. Although form in fiction is a reality, as we have seen, its possibilities are manifold. The author, accordingly, can express himself with extraordinary freedom and can imprint upon his work the stamp of his own personality.

The soul is form and doth the body make

is quite as true of prose fiction as of the poetry which Spenser had in mind, and perhaps even more obviously true, though it has less often been remarked.

This, however, and everything I have said about the revelation of the writer through what he writes holds only for books that are truly original. A great deal of fiction has been written in the past, is written nowadays, and doubtless will continue to be written, which may be termed—without implying any scorn of it—derivative rather than original. With very few exceptions such great romancers and novelists as have met with popular success in their own time have influenced a group of followers, sometimes to conscious imitation but more often to a discipleship of which they have not been fully aware. This may show itself variously: in choice of material, in the way that material is viewed, in the manner the story is handled, or in style. Or, to take another case, of two authors writing in the same tradition and observing much the same conventions, one will so transcend the type as to make of it the instrument of his personal genius, while the other merely follows the fashion and produces completely unoriginal work.

Such derivative fiction may be very well written and perfectly serious in artistic intent. It may be at the time of publication quite as readable as more original productions. Indeed, the critic or the gentle reader may be excused for not distinguishing it from things of sounder value. It is ephemeral, not having the stuff of life in it, but it gives pleasure at the moment. It does one further service. Because so responsive to the fashions of the day it becomes very useful to the historian of literature, who can trace the dominant tendencies of an era more clearly by means of it than by looking only at work of lasting value. One should not despise it, but should see it for what it is. Inevitably most novels published from year to year fall into this class. Honest pieces of craftsmanship though large numbers of them are, they have not in kind or degree the qualities that make fiction independent of passing modes.

What, then, are these qualities? Why is it, to take a specific example, that the novels of Mrs. Charlotte Smith, whose works were popular at the end of the eighteenth century when Miss Jane Austen could find no bookseller ready to publish *Pride and Prejudice*, survive only to be read by the curious student, while Miss Austen's repute has mounted from decade to decade? Mrs. Smith was an intelligent woman with far greater opportunities for observing the world than Miss Austen. Before beginning to write, she herself had experienced vicissitudes that must have given her an emotional range beyond that of the dutiful daughter in the Hampshire vicarage. She was keenly alive to public and national affairs, as Miss Austen was not. She had, as her novels show, considerable insight into the characters of men and women. She also wrote a fluent and not unattractive style. Like Miss Austen she could focus a story by means of a central theme. Her *Marchmont*, for instance, illustrates fortitude, as Miss Austen's *Persuasion* illustrates pliability of temper. Thus summed up, Mrs. Smith, it might appear, ought to be regarded as a worthy rival of Miss Austen, which is far from being the case. Her novels are dead things, while Miss Austen's are making a bid for immortality.

The point is that she lacked precisely the virtues that make us speak, in our enthusiasm, of the divine Jane. First of all, she had not that extraordinary sense of form, which enabled Miss Austen to tell her stories and show her characters with such neatness, wasting no scene and moving her people forward from event to event with a firm hand. No matter how trivial the occurrence she was depicting, she gave it interest by making it a link in the close sequence through which the theme was developed. Mrs. Charlotte Smith, being no genius but merely an intelligent and industrious writer, lacked also the power of letting her characters reveal themselves through their talk as Miss Austen's do, the witty displaying their wit, the foolish their folly, the malicious their malice, the tedious the qualities that bored their acquaintance. Mrs. Smith had a shrewd notion of what her imagined people were like, but she could not synthesize them and bring them life. She failed to integrate them as personalities, and she failed to give them the stamp of her own personality. She was, in short, a writer of what I have called derivative fiction.

Neither Jane Austen nor she, it will be observed, invented the novel of domestic manners. The pattern was already in existence. Miss Austen's originality did not depend on her avoidance of established conventions or her discovery of new material for fiction. Indeed, her range of observation was more limited than that of many another author in the same tradition, who, like Mrs. Charlotte Smith, is now forgotten. Her imagination was stimulated by the kind of people she knew and the kind of incident she had encountered, and about them she wove her tales. Part of their glory comes from her unerring craftsmanship, but even more of it from her gift of seeing her material with a penetrating eye and of so representing it that it comes to us a century and a quarter later with all the freshness of contemporary work. Just how it was that she combined such clear vision with such power of expressing what she saw, we do not know. Genius, I need not say, never has been satisfactorily explained.

Let me illustrate the difference between original and derivative fiction by another example. In the seventies and eighties of the last century Thomas Hardy had his immense success with a series of novels strong in emotional power: melodrama drenched with an atmosphere that enforced by its beauty the crises through which not altogether soundly imagined characters were brought to their predetermined ends. Although Hardy has been praised for the wrong reasons more frequently than any of the other Victorians, he was a writer of fecund genius whose greatness cannot be denied. It was not strange that he should have made a deep impression on younger authors who lacked his gifts. Not only did he have an immediate disciple in Mr. Eden Phillpotts, a very capable novelist who laid his earlier stories in a county adjacent to Hardy's Wessex, but he helped to establish the vogue for regional fiction, emotionally heightened, which became very fashionable in the nineties and continues to be enthusiastically produced and read. I do not say that Hardy invented this kind of novel. One and another of its devices can be traced back through the nineteenth century to the end of the eighteenth. He did a good deal, however, to standardize it.

What I wish to point out is the difference in value between Hardy and most writers of such fiction who have succeeded him. He is not great because he discovered what he called Wessex. He is not great because of any new means of presenting human figures. In his handling of conversation he is feeble, and in the adaptation of incident to character sometimes peculiarly inept. Yet in his power of conveying a sense of the terror in nature he has not been surpassed. This profundity of feeling, which he knew how to communicate to his readers, made him a great and original writer. He revealed certain aspects of life with compelling force, using means suitable to his purposes and leaving upon everything he produced the mark of his strong personality. Others, employing the same formula, have done work of only secondary importance because they have lacked the one essential quality. Often they have used landscape as pure decoration, when it has been quite unessential to the story, or they have sentimentalized it. In one way or another they have failed, through some lack in themselves, to lift their novels out of the class of derivative fiction.

It comes to this: neither innovation and the avoidance of old devices can make an author great, nor yet any careful following of traditions that have proved admirable in the past. Some of the most eminent novelists have had no gift for inventing new methods of story-telling and have been content to follow well-trodden ways. Smollett in the eighteenth century, Mrs. Gaskell and Trollope in the nineteenth, are examples of this. Their books have lasting worth, not because they were pioneers in craftsmanship, but because they were able to represent in convincing fashion men and women as they appear to most other men and women. Their works are completely their own, moreover, bearing the unmistakable stamp of their personal qualities. On the other hand, though Horace Walpole in writing *The Castle of Otranto* hit upon something that has affected the course of fiction ever since, he was only an awkward amateur and his romance an essentially ridiculous tale.

At a day when we hear much about experimental novels, it is well to remember that there is no peculiar virtue in new devices of narrative, just as there is no danger that the romance and the novel will die if new ways are not found. We are right in welcoming all experiments in form, because every thriving art must be the product of people who are trying hard to express what they themselves see and feel; but we should not on that account be misled into thinking that the new way is necessarily a good way, or the book embodying it a masterpiece. We may well question, for example, whether the best method of representing human beings in action is to attempt to report the sequence of thoughts that flash through their minds—what has come to be known as the stream of consciousness. Though the device is extremely useful within limits, it is open to the most tedious abuses; and certainly it is not the ultimate discovery in novel writing. Those who praise it forget that character revealed by what people do or suffer always must be the essential element in a novel. To this everything else is subordinate. Only such individual responses as have interpretative value have any importance whatever in a story. I have pointed out elsewhere that an author who records the helter-skelter of his characters' thoughts and feelings is in gravest danger of failing to achieve dramatic projection of them, and of attributing his own stream of consciousness to all his people, which defeats at once the end he has in view. Although we rightly expect to find the mark of the writer on all the figures he draws, the characters must have individual being in themselves.

One may speak with even more assurance about certain recent experiments with time in fiction. Such an attempt as Mrs. Virginia Woolf's *Orlando* could not well be anything but a failure, since it did not present an imaginatively conceivable story, and it was not saved by ignoring time and space. Its novelty caught the attention of readers for a moment, but novelty never can give real worth to an unsound piece of work. By the same token Mr. Jules Romains is not necessarily an important novelist because he is trying to represent simultaneous actions, and thus to give a sense of the world as it is. He has won a considerable acclaim by the bold announcement of his purpose; but he has done little if anything more than was accomplished somewhat clumsily in the conglomerate novels of the nineteenth century. He has been widely read, I think, because he has followed a safe old formula for gaining immediate popularity—sentimentalized eroticism.

What I have been saying about novelties in craftsmanship holds true of the discovery of new material for fiction. We rightly welcome every un-exploited vein that is opened, because the variations of human nature are as astonishing as its constants; and we never know what may be revealed by a novel combination of event and setting. Yet *Huckleberry Finn* is not great because Mark Twain was the first to write fiction about people in a little town on the banks of the Mississippi. It is a book of lasting worth for a variety of reasons, the chief among them being that the author presented in it certain aspects of the universal boy more strikingly than anyone had done before, and presented them in such a way that they hold good irrespective of the setting. It is true that Mark Twain could not have placed his people elsewhere and achieved the same result, but the virtue of the tale lies not in its novelty but in its truth.

Undoubtedly a good deal of the excitement aroused by *Jane Eyre* when it appeared was caused by Charlotte Bronte's picture of her heroine, a plain girl of good mind and extreme candor, who dared avow her passion for a man before she had married him. In 1847 that sort of thing was startling to novel readers, and it shocked many of them. It shocks nobody now, but the novel remains a penetrating study of a human being, who can capture the imagination as completely to-day as she did nine decades ago. Again, the book was not good because the material was new, but because it was a superb and highly personalized treatment of a theme that has lasting interest.

Walter Scott is another novelist who opened a new field but did not depend on this for his greatness. As a matter of fact, one of the astonishing things about Scott was his power of dealing equally well with material from very different sources. His admirers would agree that stories like *Old Mortality* and *The Heart of Midlothian* are greater than those like *Ivanhoe* and *Quentin Durward*; yet the world could ill spare the kind that is less precious. In both veins he was a pioneer, but in both he was a master, which is a fact of far greater importance. His deep understanding of the human heart and his gift of weaving incidents into an enthralling pattern were present in all his work. He is neither greater nor less great because of his position in the history of the English novel.

The same thing may be said with even more truth about Henry Fielding. He not only invented the mechanism with which he worked, but brought it close to perfection; he not only discovered fit material for use, but he used it so well that he has not been surpassed in his art by any later novelist. Were he merely a pioneer, he would have become long since a dim figure in a text-book, whereas he is more widely appreciated to-day than when Gibbon—not wont to be over-enthusiastic—called him "our immortal Fielding."

In one way only, perhaps, is the discovery of new material of really great importance to a novelist or romancer. It may well be that his observation will be quickened and his imagination stimulated if he has turned to scenes of human life that have not before been the subject of fiction. Undoubtedly Mark Twain did his best work when he dealt with a way of life that was unknown to most of his readers, even through stories, but known so well to him that he could treat it with the freedom of intimacy. It was matter peculiarly apt for his use. An eye kept fresh to see and an imagination fired by what is seen are of paramount importance, after all, to the making of significant fiction. The novel scene has some importance, as I say, yet it will not furnish an author with keen vision or provide him with imagination. If he has these requisites, however, all places will serve him, no matter how often used before. Chaucer's pilgrims went to Rochester, and so did the members of the Pickwick Club. The writer of lesser degree may keep from imitating his betters, or copying a familiar formula, by discovering a corner of the earth for his own cultivation; but the man or woman of unusual talent needs no such protection.

For her or for him, experience seems to indicate, problems of elemental and therefore permanent interest may be suggested quite as well by scenes and human types familiar to fiction as by those never before observed. Precisely the same thing is true of material as of craftsmanship: nothing is stale which is illuminated by the great artist. He will not see it as it has been seen before, or understand it as it has been understood. The reality that he envisages will be different from that of his predecessors, and his treatment of it will be his own. The fear, sometimes expressed, that the novel will perish because in due time all possible situations will have been explored, does not take into account this constant renewal. There are very few plots in the world, no doubt, but they have been used for a great while and will serve for many centuries yet to come. The variety of human nature is so infinite that the old story becomes a new one when told by a master of the craft.

Yet it would be false to say that the theme does not matter—that there is no scale of values in fiction beyond those based on the skill of the author and his particular human wisdom. It is not true that all good romances are equally good and all good novels of equal worth. Although we cannot measure the elements, as chemists do, and arrange a neat set of molecular weights, we are aware of differences. The difficulty about assessing them is this: the excellences of one masterpiece of fiction are not fairly comparable with those of another. One novel, for example, gives us subtly drawn portraits, from which we can learn much about motive and the clash of instinct with instinct; another presents the complex spectacle of many individuals acting and reacting as a social group; still another with an even larger canvas shows us the interlocking circles of several groups. There are great novels which represent the surfaces of life with such precision that we can relive the events through which the characters pass; there are others in which the depths of passion are profoundly stirred. Both comedy and tragedy are within the province of the art.

With so many imponderables to take into account, the attempt to set up a hierarchy of fiction would be futile. We may admit that stories serving no other end than to give us self-forgetfulness or mental exercise belong to a lower kind. Of this sort is the adventure tale that touches none of the major instincts and aspirations of mankind but merely excites our nerves, or the mystery yarn that excites and puzzles us, or the love story that plays with sentiment. They give us amusement and make no serious pretensions. Apart from them, however, an arrangement of fiction in neatly evaluated categories cannot be attempted.

Qualitatively the differences even among novels of the superior sort are so pronounced that it is impossible to say with conviction, for example, whether *Pride and Prejudice*, with its beautiful craftsmanship, should be set above *Wuthering Heights*, with its emotional intensity; or whether Emily Bronte, on the other hand, is greater than Jane Austen. The critic is rash who will assert that Meredith is better than Hardy, or Hardy better than Meredith. If he does so, you will find on examination that he is guided by prejudice and individual predilection rather than by sound argument.

It is equally difficult to make any exact quantitative measurement. The broad canvas may show fewer varieties of men, and show them less completely, than the one of narrow limits. Trollope humbly doffed his cap to George Eliot for some such reason, though it is not quite clear that he need have done so, since his work had certain merits that hers did not possess. One author has a wider gamut of emotional sympathy than another, yet may not be able to represent so well the shadings of human character. The possibilities of difference in range are endless, precisely as they are in quality. There is no use in our attempting to measure such complex variables.

The difficulty of establishing a hierarchy is increased by the sad fact that no faultless romancer or novelist has yet appeared in any literature. Stories are written for men and women, about men and women, by men and women. No one can command so much skill and human wisdom that he will not fail of perfection in one way or another. Fiction is an exceedingly complex art. No one can master it completely. All the greatest practitioners have had their limitations of understanding or taste. Fielding could not appreciate—much less picture—certain aspects of feeling that Richardson drew with minute but unwavering strokes.

Jane Austen's range of performance was limited by her narrow experience. Scott, as he was well aware, sometimes failed to make his plots develop from character and never learned to order them neatly. Dickens was capable of drivelling sentimentality as well as noble sentiment, and he failed to understand many people and many things that he had observed. Stendhal presented a view of life too much narrowed by his prejudices, while Victor Hugo was equally fallible in other directions. Thackeray did not escape some of the foibles of the Vanity Fair he pictured. Balzac sometimes oversimplified human motives. But there is no need of continuing the list. All the masters have their defects, which complicates still more the problem of making any exact estimate of their relative merits.

Yet differences of value exist, which may be recognized even though they cannot be exactly assessed. The wisdom and power of Scott, his intellectual and emotional range, give him a higher place, I believe, than the very exalted seat to which Jane Austen may confidently be assigned. Charlotte Bronte's firmer hold on human life and character makes me think her even greater than her great sister. Thackeray, despite his limitations, accomplished something beyond the reach of Trollope, which is not to say that Trollope does not deserve the heartiest admiration. Even such vague estimates as these, however, are open to dispute. Until we can anatomize life itself, we shall not reach a wholly accurate critical judgment of fiction, which is at its best a counterpart of life. Each of the great romancers and novelists has comprehended some aspect of that life, and has represented it for our instruction and delight. The treasure they have laid up for us is very rich; and there is no present sign that the lode from which they have dug is failing. Men and women are still looking out at the world and giving us their interpretations of what they see. This they will continue to do, and some of them will be masters of their craft.

(6)

Why Read Fiction?

ACCORDING to reminiscences jotted down in her old age, one of my grandmothers made a curious and what seems to me an unfortunate vow in the year 1826 or 1827. She would have been at the time twelve or thirteen years old. One morning she sat down to spin in the east chamber of the New Hampshire farmhouse where she passed her girlhood, but instead of keeping to her task she took up Mrs. Radcliffe's *Romance of the Forest*. She was so "enchanted"—to use her own word—that she neglected her spinnning altogether and even failed to respond promptly when she was called to dinner. Presumably she finished the story. At all events, her conscience finally awoke. She threw the book on the bed, and resolved never again to read a novel. Thus, she recalled in later years, she found time to read "serious" books—history and the like.

Why Read Fiction?

My grandmother grew up to be an able and interesting woman, who had a wide experience of life in the course of her ninety years, but she never read another work of fiction. Possibly she gained something by her abstinence, though I do not know what. On the other hand, I am sure that she missed a good deal, and I believe that an analysis of what she missed will serve very well as a defence of reading stories. Someone may say that in our day fiction needs no defence, since everyone reads it as a matter of course. Although this is true, a consideration of its value is not out of place, since the tendency to view it with suspicion still crops up at times. The attacks by serious-minded folk, who used to feel that it ministered to the lust of the flesh and the lust of the eyes and the pride of life, no doubt have ceased; but the intellectually serious-minded sometimes treat it with a certain condescension even now. They are not quite sure whether it has the dignity of other forms. Fiction has been, indeed, the Cinderella of the arts. If we believe in its worth, we must be prepared to show that it has real values. Quite without any regard to attack or condescension, we ought indeed to set in order our ideas about the matter.

The simplest use of fiction, and probably the earliest one, is to amuse and to give release. My grandmother wrote of being "enchanted" by *The Romance of the Forest*, by which she meant that she became so absorbed in it that she forgot time and her duty. Children are thus enchanted by the stories told them, or read to them. In all countries and all times folk-tales have worked their spells, and brought self-forgetfulness as well as enjoyment to the listeners. There is a certain virtue, I suppose, even in the manufactured romances produced and published in quantity nowadays. The business man finds release in the tales of adventure of the pulp magazines; the housewife in the sentimental fiction made by formula, which she reads in periodicals of every degree. There is a large public for the puzzles offered by detective stories, some of which add to their appeal by recourse to the horrific. Enchanted by such tales, some of them well made and some ill, we are set free from time and place, and get relaxation that is very grateful to our nerves. Fiction so made and so used is simply a narcotic, as we have observed already, harmless if not taken in too large doses or too often. Though my grandmother did not think so, it is good for us now and then to forget our spinning.

But romances of the better sort, and novels too, may give us release of another and higher kind. We may by means of them find an outlet for our emotions that has positive value. If we let ourselves become absorbed in the sufferings and joys of others, in their escapes and destinies, the experience is definitely sanitative. Aristotle, having observed the effects of tragedy, wrote of a purgation through pity and terror. A cleansing of the same kind may come also through comedy, and through narrative as well as drama. There can be a purgation of joy fulfilled; there can be a purgation of humor. Epic poetry gives this experience of emotional release in a high degree, and noble romance in verse may do so. It may come, too, from reading prose fiction, provided the fiction has certain indispensable qualities, and it is something quite real. The imaginative exercise of the emotions does have a healing and cleansing effect. Who is not better and saner for having read Sir Walter Scott? Who is not stronger to face the world for having lived through the stories told by Dickens? Can there be any doubt of the purgation that comes from reading *Treasure Island*? It is not a matter of noble heroes performing noble deeds; on the contrary, books dealing with problems of evil are quite as likely to give us the experience as are those that dwell upon virtue. We get it, surely, from *Wuthering Heights*. If not all fiction of the superior sort provides it, the fault lies not with the art but with the artist.

Another value that fiction may have for the reader is to give him what I have called in earlier chapters vicarious experience, by which I mean something quite different from the emotional experience just discussed. No one of us individually could go far towards understanding the world in which we live. Without the knowledge that has been collectively gathered for ages, and collectively preserved, we should be helpless creatures indeed. Our state would be far worse than that of the infant crying in the night, who has long been our symbol for utter desolation. We should know very little about ourselves, less about other people, and practically nothing about the surrounding universe.

Natural science, the result of a collective endeavor that began before the days of Greek activity and that has proceeded at an ever increasing tempo during the past three centuries, tells us about the constitution and workings of the physical world. Philosophy gives us the collective though conflicting speculations of thoughtful men about the human race and the cosmos. Psychology tries to solve the riddle of our thoughts and feelings, as well as our actions. The social sciences, as we call them, deal with the behavior of men in groups and with the history of their behavior. All these fields of study have been invaluable aids to our knowledge of ourselves and others, no less than of our environment.

You will note, however, that except for biography as an adjunct and component of history, these intellectual efforts treat man as a phenomenon of existence rather than as a person. It is on this account that fiction has a place of peculiar importance. It has served and continues to serve as an educative force inestimable in value, which seldom is recognized. Time out of mind, our common ancestors have observed themselves and others, have stored up intuitive perceptions, have used their imaginations, and have told stories embodying the traditional wisdom of the race. The process has been wholly unscientific of course, wholly unsystematic. Because of this, fiction never has been free from error and prejudice. It has perpetuated superstition and often darkened counsel. This we must admit, though we do well to remember that science and history have not been free from similar faults. Taken all in all, fiction has done infinitely more good than harm by collecting and preserving traditional experience. When we hear or read stories, we gain vicariously some of the wisdom which the imagined characters come to and pay for by blood and tears; and they in turn could not be shaped as they are if there were not behind them a vast store of intuitive knowledge available to their authors.

Without in any way minimizing the value of narratives in verse, we must recognize that prose is the medium commonly used in recent times by story-tellers to provide us with the vicarious experience that we are considering. In some ways verse is a finer vehicle of expression than prose, and very likely a noble epic is a higher achievement in literature than a great novel. Epics and verse romances certainly have done much to civilize the race. It so happens, however, that we commonly look to prose fiction nowadays for our pictures of life.

At this point it is well to observe that the vicarious experience of action is a somewhat different thing from the vicarious experience of character, though the two may come to us simultaneously from the same story. When we read tales that interest us by their plots, irrespective of the people to whom the events happen, we tend to lose for the time our consciousness of ourselves. It is the nature of romance, as I have shown earlier, to lead

Why Read Fiction?

us to identify ourselves with the heroes and heroines and to enter into their lives. In so far as significant experience can discipline and teach an individual, we are disciplined and taught. Since the experience comes to us as if it happened to us personally, we store it up among the impressions gained through contact with the real world. To sail with Jim Hawkins, when boys, is to get at least a modicum of the resourcefulness and sense of moral values that he acquired. To wander with Kim across India is to gain something from the discipline that moulded him. Apart from emotional release, then, tales of action give us contacts imaginatively with many things which we should not otherwise meet, and the wisdom coming from such experience.

But even simple tales seldom fail to provide the other sort of vicarious experience, since most stories of real worth during the past century have included a certain amount of solid characterization. *Kim* is a story of adventure, but it is peopled with individuals who become intimately known to us. To wander with young O'Hara is to wander with the Lama, and to learn about him and from him as Kim did. What is more, it is to become his friend. No one, even though favored with a wide circle of acquaintance, can know well a great number of persons in a lifetime. Opportunity fails, and leisure, besides which most of us lack the ability to penetrate the masks that others wear. Through fiction our circle of friends can be endlessly enlarged. We learn to know the people in books, moreover, under expert guidance. The author not only tells us what they do but what they think and feel, and what motives impel them. Sometimes he does this by straightforward explanation but more often by placing them in situations which sharply define their qualities. Whatever their creator knows about them we may hope to know, and whatever human wisdom he has may be ours.

It is true that all authors, even those of keenest observation and sharpest intuitions, are fallible in knowledge and the power of representation. The imagination of a Fielding or a Balzac sometimes falters and falsifies. Yet the insight of the masters of fiction is so much better than that of the ordinary reader that it is more becoming in us to admire their successes humbly than to carp at their failures. Apart from their native gifts, they have made good use in most cases of the work of their predecessors, which has taught them much. The sum of traditional knowledge about human nature, partly incorporated in literature and partly inherited among other instincts that come to the surface in curious ways, is more considerable than we often recognize. No doubt the native gifts of great novelists, to which I have just referred, depend in large measure on their being able to use this buried lore. Their intuitions are peculiarly keen, as are their powers of observation.

Although they are fallible, they give us the opportunity to acquire a vast amount of vicarious experience through what they have written. All sorts and conditions of men are shown to us, the highest and the lowest, the noble and the mean. Consider the range of characters, for example, that we find in the Waverley novels alone: from Louis of France to Dandie Dinmont or Meg Merrilees. Do we not know English people of the eighteenth century rather intimately after reading Fielding and Richardson, Smollett and Sterne, Miss Burney and Miss Edgeworth? Trollope peopled London and Barsetshire richly; and equally rich in characters is the work of the other Victorian giants. From Conrad and James we get an intimate knowledge of the mental and emotional attitudes of the people whom they studied. We learn from Hawthorne and from Melville how the hearts of men may be tortured by passion and remorse. Or we may turn the pages of Lady Murasaki and acquaint ourselves with the inner life of the Japanese aristocracy when

King Cnut ruled England. The variety and extent of all this are past computing.

The vicarious experience of character obtained from fiction differs from the vicarious experience of action in another way also. We receive it with a different attitude. However much we may be enthralled by a story in which characterization is important, we learn to know the people with a certain detachment. We are less self-centered than is the case when we are reading a romance. We move about among the figures of the tale, look into their minds and hearts, but remain ourselves. Because we stand somewhat aloof as spectators we are able to concentrate our attention on their qualities, and thus enlarge our knowledge of human nature. It is almost as if we ourselves, provided always that we read with our imaginations awake, were actually present while the events took place and with unsealed eyes could observe the participants.

From the knowledge of others gathered through this experience we learn, or ought to learn, to know ourselves the better and so approach the heart of wisdom. Our perceptions, our judgment, our sympathies will be strengthened to the extent that the experience occurs, since our apprehension of others must go hand in hand with our apprehension of ourselves. It is not a fantastic hope that the discriminating reader of fiction will be a keener yet kinder observer of his fellows, and a more candid critic of himself, than the person who never has exercised his imagination in this way.

The emotional release and the vicarious experience that we have been considering are, I believe, the primary objects in reading stories, and they furnish an adequate defence of the practice. There is a secondary and subordinate end, however, which is the acquirement of ideas and information. In discussing the place of abstract problems in fiction, we have seen that there is a hazard for the author who introduces them. He must either write some sort of apologue or else develop his theme in such a way that the ideas are evoked by the situations in which the characters find themselves. To treat the novel as a mere vehicle of propaganda, discussion, or the dissemination of knowledge is to spoil it as a means of interpreting human character. It is not a substitute for history, or sociology, or psychology, or philosophy, but has dignified uses of its own. Yet if the proper values are observed, it may picture the world, and many elements in the world, more justly and more effectively than they can be shown in a treatise. It may give us ideas, and it may give us information.

Things as they are and things as they have been in the past can equally well be presented for our instruction. We should remember, furthermore, that the fiction written yesterday about contemporary life becomes the most accurate sort of historical fiction to-day. The *Princesse de Clèves*, for example, shows extremely well how people thought and behaved at the court of Louis XIV, even though Mme. de la Fayette ostensibly used another scene. By means of novels, again, we have an incomparable record of English life extending from the middle of the eighteenth century to the present. And does not such a book as *Huckleberry Finn* preserve for later generations a phase of American life already remote from us?

One peculiar virtue of fiction, from the point of view of the reader, is the easy and familiar association with the author that it may provide. In the last chapter I discussed this matter with reference to the making of stories, but I ought to mention it again while we are summing up the advantages that the reader enjoys. Sometimes we get on similarly intimate terms with the writer through narrative verse, but less often than through prose fiction. Of all things made by the art of man, I should suppose, this brings us in closest touch with those who have produced it—some of the wisest in their generations. Theirs has been the wisdom of humanity, traditional, intuitive, based on observation of reality and ripened by time. It is a privilege to be on terms of such freedom with them, and this privilege all of us share.

In what I have been saying I have made the assumption that we have in mind fiction of some merit, as good at least—let us assume—as the book that my grandmother flung aside. Although trash is harmless in moderate doses, a steady diet of it causes fatty degeneration of the brain. It is possible to go on such a spree of detective stories that one sickens of them, or to become such a chronic toper that his state is like that of the confirmed alcoholic. It is possible to debauch oneself on the kind of stories usually printed in women's magazines, and be left with distorted ideas, perverted emotions, and an imagination totally limp. The worst of such abuses of narcotic fiction is that one's taste may be permanently injured. There are people, strange as it may seem, who can find no pleasure in Scott and yet can read the *Saturday Evening Post*. The fault, obviously, is not Sir Walter's. A vitiation of normal and natural taste like this is not only deplorable but quite without excuse.

How to Read Fiction

In estimating the benefits of fiction to the reader, as well as its possible disadvantages, it would not be candid to ignore certain aberrations from decency that the novel has suffered in our time. Authors who have taken themselves seriously—and who have been accepted more or less at their own valuation—have kicked over the traces of decorum in the name of truth. A perusal of their works leads to the conviction that they have done so less from a devotion to reality than from a desire to show themselves emancipated from the foolish pruderies by which their forbears were shackled for two or three generations. The vogue of obscenity doubtless has been useful as a revolt, but it has not resulted, as far as I can determine, in any special merit in the books produced under its influence. A novelist must be free to picture the world as he sees it, but he ought to see things in right perspective. A cult of any kind, whether of gentility or of pornography, is sure to be very bad for his work. D. H. Lawrence was as unfortunately hobbled as W. D. Howells. The reader who turns to fiction for some enlargement of experience and some quickening of mind cannot afford to be squeamish, since things both sordid and evil must be shown in any comprehensive vision of life; but he need not be misled into thinking that because a story is peppered with formerly unprintable words it is on that account a great work. Coleridge's dictum about *Tom Jones* probably suggests as good a criterion in this matter as could be found. He said, you will remember, that any youth who could be injured by reading the book was already so hopelessly corrupt that we need not be troubled about it. *Tom Jones* is neither made nor marred by Squire Western's vulgarities of speech, but is better for the presence of Squire Western.

I believe it to be true, as I have said, that great fiction of many kinds has a cleansing and healing effect through the emotional release that it affords. Beyond this, it may be a definite stimulus to virtue, not by didacticism and moral tags, but by and of itself. The *Haec fabula docet* is unnecessary and indeed intrusive: if the story itself does not incite the reader to right thinking and the good life, no comment of the author can make it do so. On the other hand, fiction like the drama may warn us against evil, may clear our minds, may stir us to noble action.

There are those who will scoff at this doctrine and protest that stories serve only for light reading and idle hours. They may be true puritans like my grandmother, whose opinion I respect though I think it unfortunate, but they are more likely to belong to the motley tribe of neo-puritans mentioned earlier, who never yet have discovered the real values of fiction. Until they learn to recognize its importance as a means of interpreting the world, there is little use in arguing with them. Untroubled by their views, the rest of us will continue to read romances and novels according to our mood.

If we are sensible readers, we shall not limit ourselves either to masterpieces that have been tested by time or to those other masterpieces issued almost monthly by ever-hopeful publishers. It would be as absurd to read only old books as to read only the new. Every generation makes something different of the fiction of the past, though it finds the most important elements unchanging; but every generation requires a fresh solution for the riddle of earth. It would be a serious mistake to neglect either the one or the other. By reading the fiction of the past we not only get human nature in a fair perspective, but we develop taste which may be exercised when we turn to the work of our contemporaries. Here we find embodied the special problems and the special preoccupations of our own time, its humors and its distresses, and we respond with eager interest to what we read. If authors of exceptional insight and imagination happen to appear, we catch aspects of truth of peculiar value to ourselves. There is every reason why to-day's fiction should appeal to us, no reason why yesterday's should be ignored.